BLITZTRAINING

ENGLISCH
Konversation

W0222835

Compact Verlag

Text: Laura W. Montgomery
Chefredaktion: Evelyn Boos
Redaktion: Brigitte Engel
Fachredaktion: Michael Hope
Produktion: Wolfram Friedrich
Gestaltung: Parzhuber und Partner – Agentur für Marketing GmbH, München
Umschlaggestaltung: Inga Koch

ISBN 3-8174-7562-4
7275621

Besuchen Sie uns im Internet: www.compactverlag.de

Vorwort

Fremdsprachen schnell und unkompliziert anwenden und vertiefen – die neue Reihe Compact SilverLine Blitztraining macht's möglich! Lernen Sie die Welt der englischen Gespräche einmal ganz anders kennen, nämlich durch den Alltag von John, Lisa und ihren Kindern Tom und Rachel.

Dieser Band trainiert die wichtigsten Themen der englischen Konversation. Vom Kennenlernen über Small Talk, Terminvereinbarungen und Flirten bis hin zu Reisen und Telefonieren – die verschiedensten Phrasen, Floskeln, Redewendungen und Idiome des Miteinander-Kommunizierens in Freizeit und im Beruf werden durch praxisnahe Beispiele auf unterhaltsame Weise vermittelt.

Ob in der Bahn, zu Hause oder im Wartezimmer – die Familie Smith und die 100 abwechslungsreichen Übungen in diesem Buch können Sie überall hin begleiten. Tragen Sie die Lösungen einfach direkt ins Buch ein. Das Pensum bestimmen Sie selbst, denn die einzelnen Übungen können unabhängig voneinander gelöst werden. Infoboxen erläutern nach und nach zuvor abgefragte Themen, die erfahrungsgemäß vielen Lernenden Probleme bereiten. Lästiges Nachschlagen in anderen Hilfsmaterialien entfällt.

Ein Verzeichnis der verwendeten Abkürzungen finden Sie auf Seite 144.

Sprechen Sie schon morgen besser Englisch – Blitztraining hilft Ihnen dabei!

Choose a word from the list to complete each sentence!

a	*Hi. You ________ be John.*	know
b	*Yes. It's nice to ________ you again.*	before
c	*It's a ________ for me too.*	mistaken
d	*What did you say your ________ was?*	doing
e	*I'm Sam. How are you ________?*	sure
f	*________ good. And you?*	time
g	*Not ________. But things could be better.*	meet
h	*Didn't we meet here once ________?*	bad
i	*I don't think so. I'm here for the first ________.*	name
j	*I see. I must have been ________.*	pretty
k	*Yes. I'm quite ________ we first met somewhere else.*	must
l	*I'd really like to get to ________ you better.*	pleasure

Lösung 2

a *I've been working a lot recently.* **b** *Yes it has, hasn't it?* **c** *Sure, you're Lisa, aren't you?* **d** *How do you do?*

Choose the correct response to each statement!

2

(a) *So, what have you been up to?*

- ❑ *I've been working a lot recently.*
- ❑ *Yes, you should stop by.*

(b) *It's been a while since we last saw each other.*

- ❑ *Yes it has, hasn't it?*
- ❑ *I'm not from here, though.*

(c) *Your face rings a bell, have we met before?*

- ❑ *I don't hear it.*
- ❑ *Sure, you're Lisa, aren't you?*

(d) *How do you do?*

- ❑ *Fine, thanks.*
- ❑ *How do you do?*

Lösung 1

a *must* **b** *meet* **c** *pleasure* **d** *name* **e** *doing* **f** *Pretty* **g** *bad* **h** *before* **i** *time* **j** *mistaken* **k** *sure* **l** *know*

Choose the correct statement for each situation!

a *John is saying goodbye to a friend who's visiting from California.*

- ❑ *I hope you enjoyed your visit.*
- ❑ *I hope you are treated well.*

b *Tom is talking with friends and remembers that he's late to meet his girlfriend, Helen.*

- ❑ *Sorry, but I really must be going.*
- ❑ *Please forgive my tardiness.*

c *Lisa is at a dinner party and is saying goodbye to a person she met there.*

- ❑ *Nice to meet you.*
- ❑ *Nice meeting you.*

d *John is saying goodbye to a business colleague and promises to call him.*

- ❑ *I am in contact with you.*
- ❑ *I'll be in touch.*

Lösung 4

a *Remain standing.* **b** *Forgive me.* **c** *You're welcome.* **d** *Ha ha.* **e** *I'll see you later.* **f** *Welcome.* **g** *Like to see you.* **h** ... **i** *Good gracious.* **j** *Do it later.* **k** *I must*

Circle the sentence that doesn't belong!

- (a) *Remain standing./Keep in touch./Stay in contact.*
- (b) *See you later./So long./Forgive me.*
- (c) *Thanks for coming./We were happy to see you./You're welcome.*
- (d) *Ha ha./Ta ta./Cheerio.*
- (e) *I'll see you to the door./I'll show you to the door./I'll see you later.*
- (f) *Cheers./Bye./Welcome.*
- (g) *Nice to see you./Like to see you./Good to see you.*
- (h) *Farewell./Do well./Goodbye.*
- (i) *Goodnight./Good evening./Good gracious.*
- (j) *Stop by later./Do it later./Come around later.*
- (k) *I must get going./I must be off./I must be mistaken.*
- (l) *Long time, no see./Haven't seen you in a while./See you soon.*

Lösung 3 **a** *I hope you enjoyed your visit.* **b** *Sorry, but I really must be going.* **c** *Nice meeting you.* **d** *I'll be in touch.*

Greetings

Some of the basic English greetings found in textbooks are no longer in common use. For instance, outside the business world you will not often hear people having the following exchange:

How do you do? How do you do?	Wie geht es Ihnen? Wie geht es Ihnen?

This is because *How do you do?* is not a real question and the correct, formal reply to this 'question' is to repeat it to the other person.

The following informal greetings are more common:

How're you doing?	Wie geht's?
Hello. How's it going?	Hallo, wie läuft's?
Hi. What's new?	Hi, was gibt's Neues?

Even if you are not doing very well, when someone asks *How are you?* the best way to respond is simply to say *Fine/Good, thanks.* ("Danke, gut."). A long explanation of your health problems is not necessary!

Nice to meet/meeting you

Remember, you say *Nice to meet you.* ("Schön, Sie kennen zu lernen.") when you are meeting someone. When you are saying goodbye to someone you have just met, you say *(It was) Nice meeting you.* ("Es war schön, Sie kennen zu lernen.").

Cheers

Cheers is an informal expression of good wishes. There are three different ways you can use it:
as *goodbye*, as *thanks* and as good wishes before drinking. In the US, *cheers* is only used in this last situation.

Cheers, John, see you later.	Tschüss, John. Bis später.
Oh, you paid for my coffee? Cheers!	Ach, du hast meinen Kaffee bezahlt? Danke!
Let's drink to our health. Cheers!	Trinken wir auf unsere Gesundheit. Prost!

5 Fill in the missing letters!

(a) – *It's a bit chilly today, isn't it?*
– *It's absolutely f_ _ _z_ _g.*

(b) – *The rain is really coming down.*
– *Yes, it's really p_ _r_ _g.*

(c) – *What a hot day!*
– *Yes, it's b_ _l_ _g.*

(d) – *Gosh, it's really warm and uncomfortable.*
– *Yeah, it's very m_g_y.*

(e) – *This is lovely weather – not too hot, not too cold.*
– *Yes, it's really quite m_ _d, isn't it?*

(f) – *I can't believe how cold it is.*
– *I know. These feel like a_ _t_c temperatures.*

(g) – *This cool breeze feels nice.*
– *Yes, it's quite f_ _ _h today.*

Lösung 6 a *6* b *10* c *8* d *9* e *5* f *7* g *11* h *12* i *14* j *13* k *1* l *3* m *2* n *4*

6 Match each word with its definition!

a	*slush*	Schneematsch	1 ◯	a storm with violent wind
b	*sleet*	Eisregen	2 ◯	a period without any rain
c	*drizzle*	Nieselregen	3 ◯	a short burst of wind
d	*hail*	Hagel	4 ◯	a severe snowstorm
e	*thunder*		5 ◯	a loud noise during a storm
f	*lightning*		6 ◯	dirty snow that is melting
g	*heat wave*		7 ◯	a flash of light during a storm
h	*fog*		8 ◯	very light rain
i	*downpour*	Platzregen	9 ◯	small balls of ice
j	*gale*	Sturm	10 ◯	a mix of rain and snow
k	*hurricane*		11 ◯	a long period of hot weather
l	*gust*	Windstoss	12 ◯	thick mist restricting visibility
m	*dry spell*	Trockenperiode	13 ◯	an extremely strong wind
n	*blizzard*		14 ◯	very heavy rain

Lösung 5 **a** *freezing* **b** *pouring* **c** *boiling* **d** *muggy* **e** *mild* **f** *arctic* **g** *fresh*

Choose the correct responses!

a *Waiter, could I have a glass of water?*

- ❑ *Of course, sir.*
- ❑ *Of course, mister.*

b *Does anyone in the class have a question about the lesson?*

- ❑ *I have a question, Miss Smith.*
- ❑ *I have a question, Madam Smith.*

c *Let me introduce you to my friend, Martin Jones. He's a university professor.*

- ❑ *Nice to meet you, Mister Professor Jones.*
- ❑ *Nice to meet you, Professor Jones.*

d *Hey, Tom! It's me, your old friend Joe Thomas.*

- ❑ *Hi, Joe Thomas. How are you?*
- ❑ *Hi, Joe. How are you?*

Lösung 8 a *Mister/Mr* b *Miss* c *Professor* d *Mrs* e *your Honour* f *Excuse me* g *Officer* h *Doctor* i *Sergeant* j *Mr President* k *ladies and gentlemen* l *children*

How should you address these people?

a) *An unmarried man – "How are you today, ___________ Smith?"*
b) *An unmarried woman – "Can I ask you something, ___________ Jacobs?"*
c) *A university professor – "Nice to see you again, ___________ Jones."*
d) *A married woman – "Hello, ___________ Smith. How are you?"*
e) *A judge – "Yes, I understand, _________________."*
f) *Someone you don't know – "_______________, could you tell me where the bank is?"*
g) *A policeman – " ___________, could you please come here and help me?"*
h) *A medical doctor – "I'm feeling just fine, ___________."*
i) *A military sergeant – "Good evening, ___________."*
j) *A male president – "Nice to meet you, _________________."*
k) *A group of people – "Good evening, ___________________________."*
l) *A group of young children – "Come and say hello to your new teacher, ___________."*

Lösung 7

a *Of course, sir.* **b** *I have a question, Miss Smith.* **c** *Nice to meet you, Professor Jones.* **d** *Hi, Joe. How are you?*

The weather

In the English-speaking world, you will often hear conversations that begin with comments on the weather. Together with health, holidays and the family, the weather is one of the most common topics for small talk.

To ask about the weather, use the question *What's the weather like?*

Comments about the current weather conditions usually begin with *It is ...*
Comments about the weather forecast are introduced with the words *They say ...*

E.g. *It's quite chilly today.*	Es ist ziemlich kühl heute.
Yes, and they say it's going to get colder.	Ja, und es soll kühler werden.

If, for example, it's cloudy and you believe it will rain soon, use one of these phrases:

It looks like rain/like it's going to rain.	Es sieht nach Regen aus.
We'll have a picnic tomorrow, weather permitting.	Wir werden morgen ein Picknick machen, wenn das Wetter mitspielt.

Forms of address

In informal situations, if two people have already met once before, they normally use first names with each other. Titles and surnames are used only in business environments or with someone you don't know well. Remember, titles in English are often simpler than they are in German. For example, a university professor with a doctorate degree is addressed as either *Doctor X* or *Professor X* – but never as *Mr/Mrs Professor Doctor X.*

Mr is used for all men, whether married or not. *Mrs* is used for a married woman and *Miss* for an unmarried woman. When you don't know whether a woman is married or not, you should use *Ms.* In addition, these days many women prefer the neutral *Ms* and in formal situations it is better to use this title.

People who provide a service will address people very formally or informally depending on the circumstances. For example, a hotel porter will refer to guests as *Sir* and *Madam*, but a taxi driver is likely to call them *Mate* or *Miss/Lady* (depending on the lady's age).

Love and *dear* are sometimes used in informal situations.

E.g. *Sorry, dear/love. I didn't see you.* Entschuldigung, ich habe Sie nicht gesehen.

Put the two dialogues into the correct order!

9

a) *It's in Maple Street now.* ◯
b) *I'm looking for a chemist's. Is there one nearby?* ◯
c) *Where is it now?* ◯
d) *No, it's just along here.* ◯
e) *You look a bit lost. Are you OK?* ◯
f) *Well, there used to be one right here, but it's been moved.* ◯
g) *Maple Street? Is that far?* ◯

a) *Go down this street and take the second turning on the left.* ◯
b) *Thanks a lot!* ◯
c) *Excuse me, I'm trying to find the post office.* ◯
d) *The second turning – where that red car is coming out?* ◯
e) *That's it. You can't miss it.* ◯

Lösung 10 **a** *to* **b** *at* **c** *between* **d** *in (engl.)/on (am.)* **e** *opposite* **f** *in* **g** *to* **h** *opposite*
i *in* **j** *at* **k** *in* **l** *between* **m** *on* **n** *to*

Complete the sentences with *in, between, to, at* or *opposite*!

a) *The bank is right next ________ the butcher's.*
b) *Turn left ________ the traffic light.*
c) *The bank is ______________ the butcher's and the bakery.*
d) *You'll find yourself ________ Maple Street.*
e) *The toy shop is directly ______________ the bakery.*
f) *The railway station is right ________ the middle of the city.*
g) *Follow this road ________ Oxford.*
h) *The post office is on the ______________ side of the street.*
i) *You can get there ________ five minutes if you walk quickly.*
j) *Leave the motorway ________ Exit 31.*
k) *You'll be standing ________ front of a huge church.*
l) *You'll see a statue standing in ______________ two large trees.*
m) *You'll see the coffee shop ________ your left.*
n) *Stop before you get ________ the end of the road.*

Lösung 9

a *5* **b** *2* **c** *4* **d** *7* **e** *1* **f** *3* **g** *6*
a *2* **b** *5* **c** *1* **d** *3* **e** *4*

Circle the correct word(s)!

11

a) *It's only a (five-minute/five-minutes) walk from here.*

b) *The railway station is about two (kilometre/kilometres) north of here.*

c) *I'm trying to find a bank. Is there one (in near/nearby)?*

d) *Just keep going (straight ahead/straightforward).*

e) *Take the first (bend/turning) on the right.*

f) *It will (take/need) about 30 minutes to get there.*

g) *Keep driving until you see (signs/signals) for Oxford.*

h) *On the (right of/right from) the bank you'll see Fox Street.*

i) *Go to the petrol station and (twist right/turn right) on Millers Road.*

j) *The city centre is (southern/south) of here.*

k) *Turn left (on/at) the crossroads and go on for 2 miles.*

l) *The bus stop is (in/at) front of the Post Office.*

m) *Go (along/through) the high street for 100 yards.*

Lösung 12

a *Du siehst aus wie scheintot.* **b** *Er ähnelt seinem Vater.* **c** *Sie ist eine sehr vernünftige Person.* **d** *Du bist kreidebleich!* **e** *Er ist seinem Großvater wie aus dem Gesicht geschnitten.* **f** *Sie ist eine echte Nervensäge.* **g** *Er ist immer eine Stimmungskanone.* **h** *Sie ist das hässliche Entlein der Familie.* **i** *Wow, bist du eine Augenweide.*

Choose the correct German translations of the idiomatic expressions!

a	*You look like death warmed up.*	◯	Sie ist eine sehr vernünftige Person.
b	*He takes after his father.*	◯	Sie ist eine echte Nervensäge.
c	*She's a very sensible person.*	◯	Er ist immer eine Stimmungskanone.
d	*You're as white as a sheet!*	◯	Wow, bist du eine Augenweide.
e	*He's the spitting image of his grandfather.*	◯	Er hat eine Stimme wie ein Nebelhorn.
f	*She's a real pain in the neck.*	◯	Du siehst aus wie scheintot.
g	*He's always the life of the party.*	◯	Sie ist nicht mehr die Jüngste.
h	*She's the ugly duckling of the family.*	◯	Er ähnelt seinem Vater.
i	*Boy, are you a sight for sore eyes.*	◯	Sie ist das hässliche Entlein der Familie.
j	*He has a voice like a foghorn.*	◯	Sie ist eine sehr sensible Person.
k	*She's no spring chicken.*	◯	Er ist seinem Großvater wie aus dem Gesicht geschnitten.
l	*She's a very sensitive person.*	◯	Du bist kreidebleich!

Lösung 11

a *five-minute* **b** *kilometres* **c** *nearby* **d** *straight ahead* **e** *turning* **f** *take* **g** *signs* **h** *right of* **i** *turn right* **j** *south* **k** *at* **l** *in* **m** *along*

13

Put the words in order from most to least flattering/extreme!

(a) ***pretty*** __________

plain __________

gorgeous __________

good-looking __________

unattractive __________

(b) ***tall*** __________

gangly __________

stately __________

long-limbed __________

(c) ***obese*** __________

chubby __________

fat __________

heavy __________

Lösung 14
a *obliging* **b** *placid* **c** *stingy* **d** *touchy* **e** *lazy* **f** *imaginative* **g** *stubborn* **h** *generous* **i** *diligent* **j** *witty* **k** *shy* **l** *affectionate* **m** *likable*

Choose the correct word to complete each sentence!

a	*John is always ready to help. He's very _______________.*	placid
b	*Lisa doesn't get excited easily. She's _______________.*	obliging
c	*She hates spending money. She's _______________.*	likable
d	*He gets upset very easily. He's _______________.*	affectionate
e	*Tom doesn't like to work hard. He's _______________.*	stubborn
f	*Rachel has many creative ideas. She's quite _______________.*	generous
g	*He's not prepared to change his ideas. He's _______________.*	lazy
h	*She donates a lot of money to charity. She's _______________.*	imaginative
i	*John works really hard. He's very _______________.*	witty
j	*Tom always tells funny jokes. He's quite _______________.*	shy
k	*Helen is quiet around new people. She's _______________.*	diligent
l	*Lisa shows her kind feelings for others. She's _______________.*	touchy
m	*Everyone enjoys being around Tom. He's very _______________.*	stingy

Lösung 13 **a** *gorgeous, pretty, good-looking, plain, unattractive* **b** *stately, tall, long-limbed, gangly* **c** *heavy, chubby, fat, obese*

Asking for and giving directions

To *ask for directions* ("nach dem Weg fragen"), say *How do I get to...?* ("Wie komme ich zu...?") or *Where is...?* ("Wo ist...?"). The most common expressions for giving directions include *turn left/right/the corner* ("rechts/links/um die Ecke biegen"), *at the next junction/set of lights* ("an der nächsten Kreuzung/Ampel").

Tip: Don't mix up *straight ahead* ("geradeaus") and *straightforward* ("einfach").

E.g. *Keep going straight ahead.* Gehen Sie immer geradeaus.
That sounds quite straightforward. Das klingt ziemlich einfach.

The verb *to be supposed to* is used like *should* to talk about something which you or other people expect.

E.g. *The bank is supposed to be around here.* Die Bank sollte hier in der Nähe sein.

When giving directions, the formula *You'll be (+ verb + -ing)* does not have a continuous meaning. It is used to describe something that can be expected to happen.

E.g. *You'll be standing opposite the bakery.* Sie werden gegenüber der Bäckerei stehen.

Describing people

Describing people involves not only talking about their appearance (*pretty, short, fair-skinned*) but also talking about their personality or character (*friendly, shy, dependable*).

The question *What's she like?* is used to ask about a person's character. The question *What does she look like?* is used to ask about a person's appearance.

The verb *describe* is followed by a direct object, which is followed by an indirect object. That is, you cannot say *Can you describe me him?* Instead, you would have to say:

Can you describe him to me? Können Sie ihn mir beschreiben?

When describing someone, it is common to use intensifying adverbs before adjectives (*extremely, unbelievably, unusually, incredibly* etc).

When describing people, English-speakers often avoid using unpleasant adjectives, such as *fat* and *ugly*. Instead, they use more euphemistic terms, such as *portly, robust* (for *fat*), or *plain, ordinary* (for *ugly*).

Pretty means attractive, but it is used only to describe women. Use *handsome* for men.

Write the time in numerals, using the twenty-four-hour clock!

15

- (a) *quarter past eleven* __________
- (b) *half seven* __________
- (c) *ten past three in the afternoon* __________
- (d) *noon* __________
- (e) *nine p.m.* __________
- (f) *two twenty-two p.m.* __________
- (g) *midnight* __________
- (h) *quarter to nine in the evening* __________
- (i) *ten minutes to ten* __________
- (j) *oh eight hundred hours* __________
- (k) *twelve a.m.* __________
- (l) *twenty past ten* __________
- (m) *one thirty p.m.* __________
- (n) *one fifteen a.m.* __________

Lösung 16 **a** *at last* **b** *in the nick of time* **c** *I'm on time.* **d** *exactly 30 minutes, less than 30 minutes* **e** *four days, forty days* **f** *after 4 p.m., by 4 p.m.*

Which expressions do not have the same meaning?

16

a *very soon*
- ❑ *in a jiffy*
- ❑ *before you know it*
- ❑ *at last*

b *very early in the morning*
- ❑ *in the nick of time*
- ❑ *at an ungodly hour*
- ❑ *at the crack of dawn*

c *I'm waiting.*
- ❑ *I'm biding my time.*
- ❑ *I'm killing time.*
- ❑ *I'm on time.*

d *a good half hour*
- ❑ *exactly 30 minutes*
- ❑ *at least 30 minutes*
- ❑ *less than 30 minutes*

e *a fortnight*
- ❑ *four days*
- ❑ *fourteen days*
- ❑ *forty days*

f *4 p.m. sharp*
- ❑ *exactly 4 p.m.*
- ❑ *after 4 p.m.*
- ❑ *by 4 p.m.*

Lösung 15

a *11.15* **b** *07.30* **c** *15.10* **d** *12.00* **e** *21.00* **f** *14.22* **g** *00.00* **h** *20.45* **i** *09.50*
j *08.00* **k** *00.00* **l** *10.20* **m** *13.30* **n** *01.15*

17

Complete each sentence with the nouns *date, appointment, meeting* or *engagement*!

a) *I won't be able to come to your party. I have a prior __________.*

b) *You're pretty. Would you like to go out on a __________ some time?*

c) *I have a __________ with my boss this afternoon.*

d) *I'm busy this evening. I've got a dinner __________.*

e) *I've got a doctor's __________ at 3 p.m.*

f) *Mr Smith is not available now. Would you like to make an __________ with him?*

g) *What's today's __________?*

h) *The investors held a __________ to discuss their investments.*

i) *My boss called a __________ to discuss the shocking news.*

j) *You want to meet tomorrow at five? It's a __________!*

k) *She had a dental __________ yesterday.*

l) *He has an __________ to perform on stage in Las Vegas!*

m) *She hasn't had a __________ with a man in years.*

n) *I'm sorry, but meetings with Mr Smith are by __________ only.*

Lösung 18 **a** *at* **b** *for* **c** *for* **d** *than* **e** *late* **f** *by* **g** *for* **h** *make* **i** *on* **j** *have* **k** *on* **l** *during* **m** *get*

Circle the correct word!

18

a) *Let's meet tomorrow morning (at/on) eight.*

b) *Do you already have plans (for/about) tomorrow afternoon?*

c) *Would you like to get together (in/for) lunch tomorrow?*

d) *Be there no later (than/as) noon!*

e) *The party starts at seven. Don't be (delayed/late)!*

f) *We're going to leave at eight, so you must arrive (by/until) then.*

g) *I've been in a meeting (in/for) the last four hours.*

h) *I won't be able to (go/make) it to the party.*

i) *Make sure you get there (for/on) time.*

j) *Let's (have/make) lunch together!*

k) *Would you like to go out (on/in) a date with me?*

l) *Why don't we meet some time (during/through) the evening?*

m) *What are you doing on Thursday? Shall we (get/come) together?*

Lösung 17

a *engagement* **b** *date* **c** *meeting* **d** *date/engagement* **e** *appointment* **f** *appointment* **g** *date* **h** *meeting* **i** *meeting* **j** *date* **k** *appointment* **l** *engagement* **m** *date* **n** *appointment*

Time

English speakers generally do not use the twenty-four-hour clock when telling the time. Instead they say either *a.m.* or *in the morning* to talk about the morning hours before 12.00 and *p.m.* or *in the afternoon/evening/night* to talk about the hours after 12.00. The twenty-four-hour clock is used at railway stations for train times and at airports for flight times and by members of the military.

The numeral *0* may be pronounced in several different ways: *zero, null, naught, oh.* When it comes to telling the time, the pronunciation *oh* is often used.

E.g. *9.05 – It's nine oh five.* Es ist neun Uhr fünf.

Be careful! *Half five* is not the same as the German "halb fünf". In British English, the word *half* refers to a half an hour after the hour.

E.g. *half five* = 5.30 "halb fünf" = 4.30

Remember that there are two translations for the preposition "seit". *Since* tells about the time that has passed between a past time and now (*I've lived here since I was young*). *For* tells about a measured segment of time (*I've been waiting here for four hours*).

Making appointments

Ask people if they have time to meet with you by asking *Are you free on ...?*
When making plans to meet with people, it is important to indicate the kind of plans you have in mind. For example, the word *appointment* ("Termin") has a neutral or service-orientated meaning. *Meeting* is used in business situations. A *date* ("Verabredung") is usually a meeting between two people who are romantically interested in each other. However, professional colleagues might arrange a *lunch date* with each other. *Engagement* ("Verpflichtung", "Verabredung") is a relatively formal expression. If you have already made plans for a certain (calendar) date and time, you might speak of having a *previous* or *prior engagement* ("schon anderweitig festgelegt sein").

I'll see you ... is a very common way to speak about future plans to meet with someone.

E.g. *I'll see you tomorrow afternoon, then.*	Also dann, bis morgen Nachmittag.

Let's do lunch is an idiomatic, informal way of saying *Let's have lunch together.*

E.g. *Are you free today? Let's have lunch together./Let's do lunch.*	Hast du heute Zeit? Lass uns zusammen zu Mittag essen.

19

Choose the word or phrase that fits best!

a	*Everything's OK, the doctor told me ________.*	flu (fam.)
b	*Don't worry, the test came back ________.*	covered
c	*Headache? Fever? You are ________ with a cold.*	sore
d	*Not to worry: If you have insurance you are ________.*	it's nothing serious
e	*You have to see a doctor fast. I'll make you an ________.*	negative
f	*Here, take one pill in the morning and one ________ bedtime.*	appointment
g	*Will I have to ________ the doctor again?*	before
h	*You'd better wear ________ clothes and stay indoors.*	coming down
i	*And make sure to rest and drink lots of ________.*	contagious
j	*I've got a runny nose and a ________ throat.*	warm
k	*You won't catch what I have – it's not ________.*	heals
l	*I was laid up in bed for a week with the ________.*	see
m	*I hope you get ________ soon.*	fluids
n	*Keep your wound clean so that it ________ quickly.*	better

Lösung 20 a *9* b *11* c *3* d *8* e *2* f *10* g *5* h *7* i *1* j *4* k *6* l *12*

Put the following dialogue in a logical order!

"Mr Smith?"

a	"Hmmm ... That's not a good sign if it's been hurting that long."	
b	"Well, it could be serious. But not if it's treated in time."	
c	"So, Mr Smith, what seems to be the problem?"	
d	"Three or four weeks ago. I'm not sure"	
e	"The doctor will see you now."	
f	"Should I be worried, Doctor?"	
g	"Do you feel anything when I do this?"	
h	"Sorry. When did you first notice the pain?"	
i	"That's me."	
j	"My stomach hurts."	
k	"Ouch! Yes!"	
l	"Well, let's find a way to treat it then!"	

Lösung 19

a *it's nothing serious* **b** *negative* **c** *coming down* **d** *covered* **e** *appointment* **f** *before* **g** *see* **h** *warm* **i** *fluids* **j** *sore* **k** *contagious* **l** *flu (fam.)* **m** *better* **n** *heals*

21

Does the colloquial exclamation express positive or negative feelings?

a) *Hooray!* __________
b) *Damn!* __________
c) *Yippee!* __________
d) *Rats!* __________
e) *Darn!* __________
f) *Whoopee!* __________
g) *Great stuff!* __________
h) *Blast!* __________
i) *Bloody hell!* __________
j) *Oh, no!* __________
k) *Oh my goodness!* __________
l) *Excellent!* __________
m) *Shit!* __________

Lösung 22
a *walking* **b** *nine* **c** *sorry* **d** *devastated* **e** *happy* **f** *sympathies* **g** *upset*
h *depressed* **i** *pink* **j** *blue* **k** *made* **l** *good* **m** *dark*

22

Complete the missing word of each English translation!

a	*Ich fühle mich wie im siebten Himmel.*	*I'm w_ _k_ _g on air.*
b	*Ich bin auf Wolke sieben.*	*I'm on cloud _ _ _ e.*
c	*Es tut mir Leid, das zu hören.*	*I'm s_ _ _y to hear that.*
d	*Ich war total niedergeschlagen.*	*I was totally d_ _ _st _ _ _d.*
e	*Ich freue mich für dich.*	*I'm very h_ _ _ _ for you.*
f	*Ich fühle mit Ihnen in Ihrem Schmerz.*	*My s_ _pa_ _ _ _s are with you.*
g	*Nimm es nicht so schwer.*	*Don't let it u_ _ _t you.*
h	*Er fühlt sich ganz deprimiert.*	*He's feeling quite d_ _ r_ _ _ _d.*
i	*Ich bin kerngesund und glücklich.*	*I'm in the p_ _k.*
j	*Ich fühle mich bedrückt.*	*I'm feeling b_ _e.*
k	*Du hast meinen Tag gerettet.*	*You've m_ _ _ my day.*
l	*Bravo!*	*G_ _d for you!*
m	*Sieh nicht immer alles so schwarz.*	*Don't always look on the d_ _k side of things.*

Lösung 21

a *positive* **b** *negative* **c** *positive* **d** *negative* **e** *negative* **f** *positive* **g** *positive*
h *negative* **i** *negative* **j** *negative* **k** *positive and negative* **l** *positive* **m** *negative*

Happiness and sadness

Expressions that have to do with happiness are usually associated with the direction *up*, the colour *pink*, and *brightness*, and *light*. Expressions that have to do with sadness are associated with the direction *down*, the colour *blue*, and *darkness*.

To ask someone about their emotional condition, ask *How do you feel?* ("Wie geht es dir/Ihnen?") If you ask someone *Do you feel like* ... you are offering that person something, e.g. *Do you feel like a cup of tea?* Möchten Sie eine Tasse Tee?

10

Sympathy

Remember, *sympathy* is "Mitleid", not "Sympathie". The most common way to express sympathy is *I'm sorry* or *I'm sorry that/to hear* … ("Es tut mir Leid.").

You can also say:	*I feel bad that* …	Es tut mir Leid, dass …
	I know what you're going through.	Ich kann verstehen, was Sie durchmachen.

11

Health

The condition of one's health and the health of one's family is a very common subject for small talk. Sicknesses that you're either *going down with* ("bekommen") or *recovering from* ("sich erholen von") are often discussed. So are illnesses that are currently *going round* ("sich verbreiten"). Remember that many body parts are associated with specific problems.

E.g. *a sore throat, runny nose, sore muscles, ear/stomach ache, headache, etc.*

Health-related comments about one's appearance are also used to start conversations between close friends and relations.

E.g. *You don't look so good.*	Sie sehen nicht sehr gesund aus.
You look great! Have you lost weight?	Sie sehen toll aus! Haben Sie abgenommen?

Your own serious illnesses are not usually discussed in small talk among acquaintances, but the serious problems of others are much discussed. It is important to know special terms in case of sudden injury or serious health problems. If a doctor asks you *What seems to be the trouble?* or *What's bothering you?* ("Was fehlt Ihnen?"), you should be able to describe the problem.

Translate the sentences and questions into English!

23

a) *Ich bin auf der Suche nach einem Rock.* ______________________

b) *Was für ein Schnäppchen!* ______________________

c) *Was steht auf dem Preisschild?* ______________________

d) *Sind die Lederstiefel zu eng?* ______________________

e) *Diese Jeans sind ausgewaschen.* ______________________

f) *Möchten Sie die Bluse anprobieren?* ______________________

g) *Sind die Absätze zu hoch?* ______________________

h) *Passt das Hemd zu den Socken?* ______________________

i) *Haben sie das Kleid in einer größeren Größe?* ______________________

j) *Ich habe diese Bluse im Schlussverkauf gekauft.* ______________________

k) *Welche Schuhgröße haben Sie?* ______________________

l) *Dieser Reißverschluss sieht kaputt aus.* ______________________

m) *Ich suche etwas Lässiges.* ______________________

Lösung 24

a *pin stripes* **b** *sales assistant* **c** *baggy trousers* **d** *business suit* **e** *knee-high socks* **f** *personal cheque* **g** *credit card* **h** *changing room* **i** *double breasted* **j** *shirt sleeves* **k** *single vent* **l** *department store* **m** *knitted ...*

Match each word on the left to one on the right!

24

a	*pin*	◯	*room*
b	*sales*	◯	*store*
c	*baggy*	◯	*jumper*
d	*business*	◯	*vent*
e	*knee-high*	◯	*assistant*
f	*personal*	◯	*trousers*
g	*credit*	◯	*sleeves*
h	*changing*	◯	*stripes*
i	*double*	◯	*card*
j	*shirt*	◯	*cheque*
k	*single*	◯	*socks*
l	*department*	◯	*breasted*
m	*knitted*	◯	*suit*

Lösung 23

a *I'm looking for a skirt.* **b** *What a bargain!* **c** *What does the price tag say?* **d** *Are the leather boots too tight?* **e** *These jeans are faded.* **f** *Would you like to try on the blouse?* **g** *Are the heels too high?* **h** *Does the shirt match/go with the socks?* **i** *Do you have this dress in a larger size?* **j** *I bought this blouse in the sale.* **k** *What size shoes do you take?* **l** *This zip looks broken.* **m** *I'm looking for something casual.*

Translate the words and use them to complete each sentence!

25

a	*This computer programme doesn't work. I'd like a __________.*	Rückerstattung
b	*This television comes with a 90-day __________.*	Garantie
c	*I've put your __________ inside the bag.*	Quittung
d	*I've finally paid all my __________.*	Schulden
e	*This CD I bought yesterday is scratched. Can I __________ it?*	austauschen
f	*How much do I __________ you?*	schulden
g	*I took out a 30,000-pound __________ at the bank.*	Anleihe
h	*I didn't have any money in the bank, so my __________ bounced.*	Scheck
i	*I'd like to open a new bank __________.*	Konto
j	*That's more than I can __________.*	sich leisten
k	*This painting is __________ over two million pounds.*	im Wert von
l	*The police stopped me for speeding. I have to pay a __________.*	Bußgeld
m	*Those shoes __________ a lot of money.*	kosten
n	*Could you __________ the money to me?*	überweisen

Lösung 26

a *paid for* **b** *sign* **c** *to* **d** *left* **e** *paid* **f** *to* **g** *per* **h** *in* **i** *leave* **j** *from* **k** *pay for* **l** *by* **m** *in* **n** *with*

Underline the correct option to complete each sentence!

26

a) *My husband (paid/paid for) the holiday.*
b) *I need a pen to (cash/sign) this cheque.*
c) *Please transfer the money (to/in) my account.*
d) *I haven't got any money (left/still).*
e) *I haven't (paid/paid for) the bill yet.*
f) *The total bill comes (to/on) 14 pounds.*
g) *The cost is ten pounds (per/every) ticket.*
h) *I'm constantly (in/for) debt.*
i) *Don't forget to (leave/pay) a tip for the waitress.*
j) *I need to borrow some money (of/from) you.*
k) *Who's going to (pay/pay for) the repairs on the house?*
l) *Can I pay (by/in) credit card?*
m) *Can I pay (of/in) cash?*
n) *He paid (with/at) a credit card.*

Lösung 25 a *refund* b *guarantee* c *receipt* d *debts* e *exchange* f *owe* g *loan* h *cheque* i *account* j *afford* k *worth* l *fine* m *cost* n *transfer*

Shopping for clothes

Most sales assistants in Britain, and especially in the US, are very friendly and helpful. When you enter a shop, a sales assistant will probably ask:

Can I help you? Kann ich Ihnen helfen?

Be careful of the differences between the verbs *suit, fit* and *match.*
If an item of clothing *suits* you, it looks good on you.
If it *fits* you, it is the right size and shape.
If it *matches* another item of clothing, they look good together. Another expression for *match* is *go with.*

In British English you *are* or *take* a certain size. You don't *have* a size.

E.g. *What size are you/do you take?* Welche Größe haben Sie?

Remember that *trousers, jeans, pyjamas* and *shorts* have no singular forms. These things always come in *pairs.* You cannot say *a trouser* – you must say *a pair of trousers.*

Tip: *Smart* ("schick") clothes are neat and fashionable in a formal way. The opposite is *casual* ("lässig"/"zwanglos"). And remember, in English, *smart* is another word for *intelligent.*

Which expression has the same meaning as the marked phrase?

a	*The prices at the resort **were exorbitant**.*	◯	*was like paradise*
b	*The package holiday's price **was reasonable**.*	◯	*was very disappointing*
c	*The view **was out of this world**.*	◯	*was perfectly clean and tidy*
d	*When we arrived, it **was high season** there.*	◯	*thought he was overly important*
e	*The holiday **was very rejuvenating**.*	◯	*was excellent*
f	*The hotel room **was immaculate**.*	◯	*wasn't too expensive*
g	*The hotel **was a rip-off** (sl.)*	◯	*were extremely expensive*
h	*The flight we booked **was a bargain**.*	◯	*was unbelievably beautiful*
i	*The holiday **was a real let-down**.*	◯	*was very refreshing*
j	*The service **was second to none**.*	◯	*were very friendly and attentive*
k	*The staff **waited on us hand and foot**.*	◯	*was high-quality and inexpensive*
l	*The waiter **was very condescending**.*	◯	*wasn't worth the money I paid*
m	*The place **was heaven on earth**.*	◯	*was the most popular time for tourists*

Lösung 27

a *on holiday* **b** *off* **c** *at* **d** *a vacation* **e** *package* **f** *on leave* **g** *sightseeing* **h** *took* **i** *sunburned* **j** *for* **k** *in* **l** *get away* **m** *break*

Rewrite the sentences that are incorrect!

29

a) *The weather was delightful!* ______

b) *I'm looking forward to getting away from it all.* ______

c) *Did you do any sightviewing?* ______

d) *How long were you away since?* ______

e) *He is a very generous host.* ______

f) *I became a very bad sunburn.* ______

g) *The holiday was filled with rest and relaxation.* ______

h) *The travel guide was very useful.* ______

i) *I took a leaded tour of the city.* ______

j) *I can't wait to go back again!* ______

k) *Our room had a great sight.* ______

l) *A day return to London, please.* ______

Lösung 30

a *I'm all packed up.* **b** *I'm taking only light luggage.* **c** *Have you checked in your luggage?* **d** *I need to change euros into pounds.* **e** *The time of arrival is four o'clock.* **f** *I can't believe you left your passport there!* **g** *We are heading off to the islands.* **h** *It doesn't take long to get to London by train.* **i** *Do you*

7

Rewrite the words in the correct order!

a) *all/I'm/up/packed/.* ____________________

b) *light/only/luggage/taking/I'm/.* ____________________

c) *have/checked in/you/luggage/your/?* ____________________

d) *need/to/I/euros into/change/pounds/.* ____________________

e) *four/time/arrival/the/is/of/o'clock/.* ____________________

f) *believe/passport/I/your/you/left/there/can't/!* ____________________

g) *islands/heading/the/we/off/to/are/.* ____________________

h) *London/take/train/it/long/doesn't/to/to/get/by/.* ____________________

i) *you/abroad/often/do/very/travel/?* ____________________

j) *to/airport/we're/taxi/a/taking/the/.* ____________________

k) *travelling/are/by/by/plane or/you/ship/?* ____________________

l) *you/long/staying/be/will/?* ____________________

Lösung 29 **a** *correct* **b** *correct* **c** *Did you do any sightseeing?* **d** *How long have you been away (for)?* **e** *correct* **f** *I got a very bad sunburn.* **g** *correct* **h** *correct* **i** *I took a guided tour of the city.* **j** *correct* **k** *Our room had a great view.* **l** *correct*

Choose the word or expression that best replaces the word(s) that are marked in each sentence!

31

a *Where are you **headed**?*

- ❑ *going*
- ❑ *coming from*

b *It was amazing - the plane **took off** right on time.*

- ❑ *departed*
- ❑ *landed*

c *My flight **was delayed for hours**!*

- ❑ *was extremely long*
- ❑ *left extremely late*

d *I did not realize my visa **had expired** until I arrived at the airport.*

- ❑ *was no longer valid*
- ❑ *was missing*

e *Darling, I bought two **return** tickets to Mexico!*

- ❑ *round-trip (am.)*
- ❑ *simple*

f *We were **stranded** at JFK for two long, cold nights!*

- ❑ *staying*
- ❑ *stuck*

Lösung 32 **a** *By car* **b** *transfer* **c** *check* **d** *have/take a break* **e** *measures* **f** *petrol station* **g** *driving licence* **h** *Simple or return* **i** *railway station* **j** *boot* **k** *departure time*

Translate the German words and phrases into English!

32

a) *How did you get there? - (Mit dem Auto).* __________

b) *We'll have to (umsteigen) at the airport in Paris.* __________

c) *They will (kontrollieren) your passport when you arrive.* __________

d) *We've been driving for hours. Let's (eine Pause machen).* __________

e) *Security (Maßnahmen) were very strict.* __________

f) *I see a (Tankstelle) up ahead.* __________

g) *I can't rent a car because I haven't got a (Führerschein).* __________

h) *You'd like to buy a ticket? - (Einfach oder hin und zurück)?* __________

i) *Can you drive me to the (Eisenbahnstation)?* __________

j) *I've put all our luggage in the (Kofferraum) of the car.* __________

k) *The (Abfahrtszeit) is half ten.* __________

l) *You'll have to make a (Flugreservierung).* __________

m) *The ticket was cheap, but had too many (Einschränkungen).* __________

Lösung 31

a *going* **b** *departed* **c** *left extremely late* **d** *was no longer valid*
e *round-trip (am.)* **f** *stuck*

On holiday

The word *holidays* is used to describe the main holidays of the year lasting a week or more. In other cases, for shorter periods, one uses the word *break*. Single days when you don't have to go to work, e.g. *Whit Monday* ("Pfingstmontag"), are called *bank holidays*.

E.g. *Where are you going for your holidays*?	Wohin fahren Sie während der Ferien?
Do you have a break coming up?	Haben Sie bald ein paar Tage Urlaub?

In the US, one says *vacation*. There, the word *holiday* means a *bank holiday*, a single day when people do not go to work.

E.g. *You don't have to come into the office tomorrow. It's a holiday.*	Sie müssen morgen nicht ins Büro gehen. Es ist Feiertag.

If you *take time off* from work ("freinehmen", "Urlaub nehmen") it means you're choosing not to go to work. Make sure you don't use the word *free* to express this. It's incorrect.

on my day off	an meinem freien Tag	*take a day off*	einen Tag freinehmen

Travelling

When asking for a ticket, people in Britain often leave out the word *ticket.*

E.g. *A day return to Oxford, please.* Eine Tagesrückfahrkarte, bitte.

When you're in an airport or railway station, people may refer to certain flights or trains by the time at which they are departing.

E.g. *Are you taking the ten thirty-five to London?* Nehmen Sie den Flieger/Zug, der um 10:35 Uhr geht?

It's always important to ask if you will have to *change* ("umsteigen"). Hopefully, if everything is *running on time* ("pünktlich sein") you won't *miss a connection* ("einen Anschluss verpassen"). It's usually a good idea to ask about any *delays* ("Verspätungen") and when you will *arrive at* or *get into* ("ankommen in") the city you're travelling to.

Be aware of the different occupational titles of the people who work in different branches of the transport industry. For example, a *ticket inspector* ("Schaffner(-in)") checks tickets on a train and a *flight attendant* ("Flugbegleiter(-in)) works in a plane.

Choose the most appropriate response to each question!

a *This tram stops at the stadium, right?*

- ❑ *I'm afraid so.* ❑ *Not really* ❑ *That's right.*

b *Will I be able to change at the next stop?*

- ❑ *Not so many.* ❑ *I believe so.* ❑ *Obviously.*

c *Busses are running ahead of schedule, aren't they?*

- ❑ *Actually, they're running late.* ❑ *Yes, they're running.* ❑ *That wouldn't be good.*

d *How much is the fare from here to Downing Street?*

- ❑ *It's faring quite well.* ❑ *Two pounds.* ❑ *About ten minutes.*

e *How many stops are left until the airport?*

- ❑ *Sure they are.* ❑ *Not very many.* ❑ *I think so, sir.*

f *Is this bus number seventeen?*

- ❑ *You should get off here.* ❑ *Not quite.* ❑ *That's right.*

g *Where does this bus stop?*

- ❑ *It certainly will.* ❑ *I have no idea.* ❑ *In a little while.*

Lösung 34 **a** *tour* **b** *repair* **c** *underground* **d** *station* **e** *direction* **f** *tube* **g** *crowded* **h** *down* **i** *turnstile* **j** *take* **k** *taxi* **l** *fare* **m** *foot*

Use the words on the right to complete the conversation!

34

a	*John: So, did you enjoy your ____________ of London today?*	underground
b	*Lisa: Terrible! All public transport seemed to be under ____________.*	direction
c	*John: What? The London ____________ too?*	turnstile
d	*Lisa: Yes. It took me an hour to even find a tube ____________.*	crowded
e	*John: Well, you don't have a great sense of ____________.*	foot
f	*Lisa: True. But things got even worse once I was on the ____________.*	down
g	*John: What happened? Was it extremely ____________?*	fare
h	*Lisa: Worse. It broke ____________.*	station
i	*John: Well, you didn't get caught in the ____________, like in New York.*	tour
j	*Lisa: Ha ha. Well, then I decided to ____________ a bus.*	take
k	*John: Why didn't you just take a ____________?*	repair
l	*Lisa: I wanted to, but didn't have enough money for the ____________.*	taxi
m	*John: Tomorrow you should go around the city on ____________!*	tube

Lösung 33

a *That's right.* **b** *I believe so.* **c** *Actually, they're running late.* **d** *Two pounds.*
e *Not very many.* **f** *That's right.* **g** *I have no idea.*

Are the marked phrases correct? Rewrite the incorrect ones correctly!

a) *Hello, I phoned yesterday* ***about two double rooms****.* ______

b) *I'd like to* ***make a reserve to*** *tomorrow night.* ______

c) *So, you're in room 262,* ***on the third level****.* ______

d) *Just take the lift* ***up three floors*** *and turn right.* ______

e) *I'll get someone* ***for you to help*** *with your luggage.* ______

f) *Do you have any rooms* ***available next weekend****?* ______

g) *Here's your room key. And this key* ***gets you into*** *the hotel.* ______

h) *Can I* ***leave my luggages*** *at the front desk for a while?* ______

i) *Does the room* ***take a view*** *of the ocean?* ______

j) *Enjoy* ***your time****!* ______

k) *Are you hungry? Let's* ***order room delivery****.* ______

l) *The ferry to Ireland* ***needs two hours****.* ______

m) *I'd like to book a room, please.* ______

Lösung 36
a *were you looking for?* **b** *to the pool and sauna areas.* **c** *May I come in?* **d** *so that's £160 in total.* **e** *the bill please?* **f** *through to room 101.* **g** *credit card details.* **h** *at the weekend.* **i** *should I make the reservation?* **j** *under Smith.* **k** *family room free next weekend.* **l** *in this form, please?* **m** *suite*

Match the beginning with the end of each sentence!

a	*What sort of room ...*	◯	*credit card details.*
b	*All guests have access ...*	◯	*in this form, please?*
c	*Room service! ...*	◯	*should I make the reservation?*
d	*OK, it's £80 per night, ...*	◯	*suite bathroom and two single beds.*
e	*Could I have ...*	◯	*at the weekend.*
f	*Could you put me ...*	◯	*to the pool and sauna areas.*
g	*I'll need to take your ...*	◯	*under the name Smith.*
h	*We stayed in a hotel ...*	◯	*so that's £160 in total.*
i	*Under which name ...*	◯	*were you looking for?*
j	*We've booked a room ...*	◯	*the bill please?*
k	*Yes, we have a ...*	◯	*through to room 101.*
l	*Could you just fill ...*	◯	*May I come in?*
m	*It's a room with en ...*	◯	*family room free next weekend.*

Lösung 35 **a** *correct* **b** *make a reservation for* **c** *on the third floor* **d** *correct* **e** *to help you* **f** *correct* **g** *correct* **h** *leave my luggage* **i** *have a view* **j** *your stay* **k** *order room service* **l** *takes two hours* **m** *correct*

Public transport

Unlike in cities such as New York or Munich, the lines of the *London Underground* ("Londoner U-Bahn") have names (e.g. *Northern Line*), not numbers. The common word for the London Underground is *the tube* (wörtlich: "das Rohr"). If you're on *the tube*, it means you're riding on an underground train between two *tube stations*.

When you are asking how much time you need to complete a trip, use the verb *take*.

E.g. *The ferry takes two hours.* Die Überfahrt dauert zwei Stunden.

While travelling to and from their workplaces, *commuters* ("Pendler") might discuss *rush-hour traffic* ("Berufsverkehr") or the ever-increasing *fares* ("Fahrpreise").

Remember to pay your fare before going through any *turnstiles* ("Drehkreuze") – otherwise you'll get in trouble for *fare-dodging* (sl.) ("schwarzfahren", sl.).

When taking a taxi, it is common to give the driver a *tip* ("Trinkgeld") at the end of the trip. For example, if the taxi fare is £ 9 and you give the driver £ 10, you can tell him to *keep the change* ("das Wechselgeld behalten").

Staying at a hotel

When you're talking about spending the night at a hotel, the word *stay* is used – both as a noun ("Aufenthalt") and as a verb ("übernachten").

Staying at a hotel usually involves a set sequence of actions: *reserving/booking a room* ("ein Zimmer reservieren"), *checking in* ("sich an der Rezeption anmelden"), *paying the bill* ("die Rechnung bezahlen") and *checking out* ("das Hotelzimmer räumen").

When you say *I'd like to reserve/book a room, please.* ("Ich möchte ein Zimmer reservieren."), you will be offered a variety of room options:

a single room	ein Einzelzimmer
a double room	ein Doppelzimmer
a twin room	ein Zweibettzimmer

You may want to check if the room has *en suite bathroom* ("eigenes Bad").
When you arrive, you will be asked to *fill in/out a registration form.* Don't confuse *form* ("Formular") with *formula* ("Formel"). You will usually be asked by the receptionist to give your *credit card details* ("Kreditkarteninformationen") to make sure you don't leave the hotel without paying your bill.

Complete each sentence with the correct word or phrase!

37

a *I'd like to put some money into an account.*
I'd like to make ______________________.

b *I'd like to take some money out of an account.*
I'd like to make ______________________.

c *I'd like to move money from one account to another.*
I'd like to make ______________________.

d *I wrote a cheque for £ 300, but didn't have that much money in my account.*
My check ______________________.

e *I didn't have enough money to pay for the amount on the cheque.*
I didn't have enough money ______________________ *the cheque.*

f *Let me know when the transferred money arrives in my account.*
Let me know when the transfer ______________________.

g *I'd like to have an account in which I can save money.*
I'd like to ______________________.

Lösung 38 a *PO* b *PO* c *B* d *B* e *B* f *PO* g *B* h *B* i *PO* j *PO* k *PO* l *PO* m *B* n *PO*

Would you hear the statements in a bank (B) or a post office (PO)?

- a) *What kind of packaging options are available?* ____
- b) *Special delivery, please.* ____
- c) *Is there a cash point in the building?* ____
- d) *I'd like to cash this cheque.* ____
- e) *May I have change for this £100-note?* ____
- f) *How much would it cost to get this to Paris.* ____
- g) *Please advise me when the transfer is complete.* ____
- h) *What's your institution's sort code?* ____
- i) *This has to be sent with overnight delivery.* ____
- j) *Is there a tracking number?* ____
- k) *What's the standard postage rate?* ____
- l) *Is there a special rate for printed material?* ____
- m) *What kind of notes would you like?* ____
- n) *I want to send it first-class.* ____

Lösung 37

a *a deposit* **b** *a withdrawal* **c** *a transfer* **d** *bounced (fam.)* **e** *to cover* **f** *comes/goes through* **g** *open a savings account*

Choose the correct word(s) to complete each sentence!

39

a	*There is no __________ on Sundays.*	bank clerk
b	*It must arrive by tomorrow. Please send it __________.*	take
c	*Did you remember to stick a __________ on the postcard?*	paper
d	*Which __________ should I send it to?*	envelope
e	*How long will the letter __________ to get there?*	rate
f	*What's the parcel __________ for something that weighs 2 kilos?*	address
g	*This must go out as soon as __________.*	postman
h	*You've forgotten to write the __________ in the upper left corner.*	first-class
i	*Don't forget to seal the __________ before you send the letter.*	post
j	*Has the __________ collected the post yet?*	sender
k	*"Return to __________"? I must've written the wrong address.*	possible
l	*Can I send this printed __________ rate?*	return address
m	*You have to ask the __________.*	stamp

Lösung 40

a *Not quite.* **b** *I feel like roast chicken.* **c** *Not for me, thanks.* **d** *We're a party of four.* **e** *Yes, that suits me fine.* **f** *Mashed, please.* **g** *Yes, sir. We've some lovely trout today.* **h** *I'll be able to seat you in ten minutes.* **i** *They're delicious!* **j** *A slice of chocolate cake, please.* **k** *Wonderful. My compliments to the*

Choose the answer that goes with each question!

a	Are you ready to order?	◯	Not for me, thanks.
b	What do you feel like having?	◯	A bottle of merlot and four glasses.
c	What about a starter?	◯	Yes, I'd like to try some.
d	A table for Friday night – for how many?	◯	A slice of chocolate cake, please.
e	Lisa, would you like to sit here?	◯	Wonderful. My compliments to the chef.
f	What kind of potatoes would you like?	◯	We're a party of four.
g	Are there any specials today.	◯	I feel like roast chicken.
h	How long is the wait?	◯	Mashed, please.
i	How's are your mussels, Tom?	◯	Not quite.
j	Anything for dessert?	◯	I'll be able to seat you in ten minutes.
k	How was everything, sir?	◯	They're delicious!
l	To drink?	◯	Yes, that suits me fine.
m	Want to try a little?	◯	Yes, sir. We've some lovely trout today.

Lösung 39 **a** *post* **b** *first-class* **c** *stamp* **d** *address* **e** *take* **f** *rate* **g** *possible* **h** *return address* **i** *envelope* **j** *postman* **k** *sender* **l** *paper* **m** *bank clerk*

Put the conversation in the correct order!

47

Waiter: Are you ready to order yet?

- (a) *Medium rare, please.* ◯
- (b) *No, no starter for me, thank you. What about you, John?* ◯
- (c) *And for your main course, sir?* ◯
- (d) *Hmm ... I think I'll have the duck, John.* ◯
- (e) *Shall we order a bottle of wine, John?* ◯
- (f) *How would you like that done?* ◯
- (g) *Very good choice, madam. Would you like a starter?* ◯
- (h) *Good idea. A bottle of your best red, waiter.* ◯
- (i) *I'll have the steak for my main course.* ◯
- (j) *Very good, sir. And finally, what would you like to drink?* ◯
- (k) *I think so, yes. Lisa, have you decided on something?* ◯
- (l) *Well, I think I'll have the soup of the day for a starter.* ◯

Lösung 42 **a** *This roast is interesting.* **b** *Have you taken a table?* **c** *I'd like my steak well done.* **d** *What will you have for dessert?*

Which word or expression does not have the same meaning as the other two?

42

a
- ❑ *This roast is excellent.*
- ❑ *This roast is delicious.*
- ❑ *This roast is interesting.*

b
- ❑ *Have you reserved a table?*
- ❑ *Have you booked a table?*
- ❑ *Have you taken a table?*

c
- ❑ *I'd like my steak well done.*
- ❑ *I'd like my steak pink in the middle.*
- ❑ *I'd like my steak rare.*

d
- ❑ *What will you have for your main course?*
- ❑ *What will you have for dessert?*
- ❑ *What will you have for your entrée (am.)?*

Lösung 41 **a** *9* **b** *4* **c** *6* **d** *2* **e** *11* **f** *8* **g** *3* **h** *12* **i** *7* **j** *10* **k** *1* **l** *5*

Bank

Many useful banking expressions are covered in "Talking about money" (page 41). If you're in a bank, you'll also need expressions like *make a deposit/withdrawal* ("Geld einzahlen/abheben").

Before giving you money, the *bank clerk* ("Bankkassierer(-in)") may ask *How would you like it?* He/She wants to know what kind of *notes* ("Scheine") you'd like to receive.

19

Post office

The *post office* is the official building in which letters and parcels are sorted. *The post* is a collective term for the letters and parcels that a person sends or receives. If you need a letter to arrive at its destination quickly, you may want to send it *first-class/express* ("bevorzugt befördern lassen"). Otherwise, send it *second-class*. If you don't know which *stamp* ("Briefmarke") to use, ask about the *letter/parcel rate* ("Porto").

20

Eating out

The expression *It's/everything is on me.* means *I will pay for everything.* ("Ich zahle."). Other ways to express this, when talking about food, are *It's my treat.*, *I'll treat you.* or *I'll take care of it.* When you are talking about drinks, the best way to express this is to say *It's my round.* When you are paying for somebody else, do not say *I will invite you.* You only say this when you're asking someone to join you for a meal.

It is very important not to confuse *menu* ("Speisekarte") with *set meal, meal of the day* or a *fixed menu* ("Menu").

When ordering, people won't normally say *I want to eat chicken.*
Don't say *I take* ...! More polite is:

I think I'll have (chicken today).	Ich denke, ich werde heute Hühnchen nehmen.
I would like (some veal).	Ich hätte gern Kalbfleisch.
I feel like (fish today).	Mir wäre heute nach Fisch.

When they have finished, British people put their knives and forks side by side on the plate. The waiter will never ask if you want a separate bill, and if he notices that you have finished eating, the waiter might bring you the bill without your having asked for it.

Translate the words and use them to complete the sentences! The first letter is already given.

43

a) *He is an excellent h__________ (Gastgeberin).*

b) *Here's a bottle of wine for the c__________/c__________ (Koch).*

c) *Who f__________ (fam.) (möchten) a glass of chardonnay?*

d) *What can I g__________ (anbieten) you?*

e) *Would a__________ (irgendjemand) like some more potatoes?*

f) *A glass of sherry would be l__________ (schön).*

g) *Everyone just h________ y________ (sich bedienen)!*

h) *Could you p__________ (überreichen) me the pepper, please?*

i) *Don't go – I was just about to o__________ (aufmachen) another bottle.*

j) *Drive c__________ (vorsichtig)!*

k) *Thanks for e__________ (alles).*

l) *I'm afraid we've got to make a m__________ (Aufbruch).*

m) *Why don't you t__________ (probieren) my wife's apple tart?*

Lösung 44 **a** *5* **b** *3* **c** *10* **d** *12* **e** *7* **f** *8* **g** *1* **h** *11* **i** *6* **j** *4* **k** *9* **l** *2*

Put the conversation in the correct order!

(The doorbell rings.)

- a *Hello, Margaret. I've heard a lot about you.*
- b *Not at all, James! Please, come in.*
- c *Mmmm ... I can already smell them.*
- d *Yes, please. I'd love one.*
- e *Same here. Why don't you both sit down?*
- f *You sit, Margaret – I'll help Lisa and John in the kitchen.*
- g *I'll go, John!*
- h *Well, while we wait can I get you something to drink? A dry sherry?*
- i *I've heard a lot about you and John too, Lisa. It's nice to finally meet you.*
- j *Thanks. I'd like to introduce my girlfriend, Margaret.*
- k *No, no, that's not necessary. John's just finishing the hors d'oeuvres.*
- l *Hi, Lisa. I hope we're not to early.*

Lösung 43 **a** *host* **b** *cook/chef* **c** *fancies* **d** *get* **e** *anyone* **f** *lovely* **g** *help yourself* **h** *pass* **i** *open* **j** *carefully* **k** *everything* **l** *move* **m** *try*

Translate the sentences and questions into English!

45

a) *Ich habe überraschende Neuigkeiten für dich.* ______

b) *Ich gehe am Sonntag zu seiner Taufe.* ______

c) *Sie wurden letztes Jahr geschieden.* ______

d) *Meine Schwiegermutter ist zu Besuch da.* ______

e) *Sie erwartet ein Kind.* ______

f) *Wann ist es soweit?* ______

g) *Wie kommt sie mit seinem Tod zurecht?* ______

h) *Bist du zur Beisetzung gegangen?* ______

i) *Er ist mit einer Amerikanerin verheiratet.* ______

j) *Sie kommen gut miteinander aus.* ______

k) *John ist der Patenonkel des Kindes.* ______

l) *Sie waren drei Jahre verheiratet.* ______

m) *Es war ein Familienanlass.* ______

Lösung 46 **a** *sister-in-law* **b** *piece of news* **c** *on* **d** *ceremony* **e** *grandchildren* **f** *sorry* **g** *gap year* **h** *getting on* **i** *up to* **j** *family man* **k** *wedding* **l** *expecting* **m** *in-laws*

Circle the correct word(s)!

- a) *My brother got married. I have a new (sister-in-law/twin sister)!*
- b) *What a wonderful (news/piece of news)!*
- c) *Oh, come (already/on)! You have to do it.*
- d) *We've just returned from the christening (ceremony/procedure).*
- e) *Do you have any (grandparents/grandchildren)? – Yes, one grandson.*
- f) *Oh, I'm (sorry/hurt) to hear that he died.*
- g) *My son's doing a (free year/gap year) before he starts university.*
- h) *How's Tom (getting on/getting forward) these days?*
- i) *What's your daughter been (on for/up to)?*
- j) *He's a wonderful father – a real (family man/parenting man).*
- k) *There were a hundred guests at the (marriage/wedding).*
- l) *She is (expecting/waiting for) twins next month.*
- m) *Does she get on with her (in-laws/outlaws)?*

Lösung 45

a *I have (some) surprising news for you.* **b** *I'm going to his christening on Sunday.* **c** *They were divorced last year.* **d** *My mother-in-law is visiting.* **e** *She's expecting (a baby).* **f** *When is it due?* **g** *How is she coping with his death?* **h** *Did you go to the funeral?* **i** *He's married to an American.* **j** *They get on well with each other.* **k** *John is the child's godfather.* **l** *They had been married for three years.* **m** *It was a family occasion.*

Entertaining at home

In English, *place* can mean a person's house or flat.

E.g. *Let's go to my place for coffee.* Lass uns bei mir eine Tasse Kaffee trinken.

What can I get you? is an informal way of asking *What would you like to drink?* Your host may ask *Would you like …?* ("Möchten Sie …?") by saying *Do you fancy …?*, which is a bit more informal. A common response to offers like these is *I'd love one …/ I'd love a …/I'd love to …* ("Ich hätte gerne …").

Guests often make polite comments about the food or drinks during a meal.

When speaking to a group of guests, a host will often remark *Help yourselves (to more)!* ("Bedient euch!"). Or, when offering something specific, like coffee, the host might say *Coffee, anyone?* ("Möchte jemand Kaffee?").

When leaving your host, it's common to say *Thanks for everything!* ("Danke für alles!"). Make sure you don't say *Thanks for all.* A host will usually respond to this expression of thanks with one of his or her own, like *Thanks for coming.* ("Danke, dass du/ihr gekommen bist/seid.").

Talking about family

If you've just been introduced to someone, you probably won't start talking to each other about your families straight away. Among friends, however, family members and their activities are common topics of conversation, including *weddings* ("Hochzeiten"), *divorces* ("Scheidungen"), *christenings* ("Taufen"), *illnesses* and *funerals* ("Beisetzungen"). These events are often discussed using euphemisms. For example:

Instead of saying *She's pregnant.* people will say *She's expecting.* ("Sie ist schwanger."). You can also say these things of a couple, e.g. *They're expecting.* ("Sie erwarten ein Kind.").

If someone is telling you about a family member or relative who lives far away, it is common to ask *Do you see much of each other?* ("Seht ihr euch oft?"). In this situation, be sure not to say *Do you see yourselves often?* If you *see yourself* it means that you are looking at yourself ("sich selbst anschauen").

When asking about how someone's family member is doing, you might ask *How is she getting on?* ("Wie geht es ihr?"). Don't confuse this question with *Does she get on with her in-laws?* ("Kommt sie mit ihren Schwiegereltern gut aus?).

Complete each sentence with the correct word!

a	*I'd like to get to ________ you better.*	run
b	*Would you like to go ________ on a date some time?*	met
c	*The drink is ________ me.*	let
d	*I couldn't help ________ you yesterday at the library.*	common
e	*Can I ________ you some time?*	say
f	*I was so glad to ________ into you again last week.*	by
g	*We seem to get on very ________. What do you think?*	ring
h	*Ah, you prefer going to the cinema. That's fine ________ me.*	time
i	*Why don't you ________ me call you first?*	know
j	*Why don't we ________ 9 o'clock at my place?*	get
k	*Well, yes, I also had a great ________.*	noticing
l	*Why don't we ________ together some time?*	on
m	*I think we have a lot in ________.*	out
n	*Haven't we ________ somewhere before?*	well

Lösung 48 **a** *fancy Rachel.* **b** *on by you, Tom.* **c** *that discourage me.* **d** *your mind?* **e** *likes you.* **f** *be friends?* **g** *for lunch together, right?* **h** *to have his way with her.* **i** *in the last row of the*

Match the beginning with the end of each sentence!

48

a	*I really …*	◯	*for lunch together, right?*
b	*I'm not turned …*	◯	*your mind?*
c	*I'm not going to let …*	◯	*likes you.*
d	*Won't you change …*	◯	*be friends?*
e	*Go and talk to her! I think she …*	◯	*on by you, Tom.*
f	*Why can't we just …*	◯	*to his advances.*
g	*We can at least go out …*	◯	*a sexy bird.*
h	*Tom keeps trying …*	◯	*fancy Rachel.*
i	*I saw them snogging (fam.) …*	◯	*tomorrow night.*
j	*Maybe she's just playing …*	◯	*that discourage me.*
k	*Go for her. She's …*	◯	*of heart.*
l	*One day she gave in …*	◯	*hard to get.*
m	*I made a date with him for …*	◯	*to have his way with her.*
n	*Rachel had a change …*	◯	*in the last row of the cinema.*

Lösung 47

a *know* **b** *out* **c** *on* **d** *noticing* **e** *ring* **f** *run* **g** *well* **h** *by/with* **i** *let* **j** *say* **k** *time* **l** *get* **m** *common* **n** *met*

Choose the phrase that has the same meaning as the marked phrase!

49

a	*Rachel was **seeing** somebody else.*	◯	stop looking at
b	*Tom regretted that Rachel **was spoken for**.*	◯	kissed
c	*Rachel **dumped** (fam.) her boyfriend after she met Tom.*	◯	said yes
d	*Tom kept trying to **pull Rachel**.*	◯	had a boyfriend already
e	*Finally, she **gave him a break**.*	◯	possessive
f	*They **smooched** (fam.) for the first time on a Saturday.*	◯	day one
g	*Tom **scored** at last!*	◯	involved with
h	*Rachel soon realized she was **wild about him**.*	◯	chat Rachel up (fam.)
i	*They were both **swept off their feet**.*	◯	got what he wanted
j	*One could say it was love from **the very beginning**.*	◯	crazy about him
k	*Things really started to **heat up**.*	◯	deeply in love
l	*Tom complained that Rachel was too **controlling**.*	◯	left
m	*Rachel couldn't **keep her eyes off** him.*	◯	get serious

Lösung 50 **a** *man* **b** *either* **c** *man (usually)* **d** *woman* **e** *woman* **f** *man* **g** *man* **h** *either* **i** *woman* **j** *woman* **k** *woman* **l** *woman* **m** *man*

Is the speaker talking about/to a man or a woman – or could it be either?

50

- **a** *I met a real hulk (sl.) at the beach.* ____________
- **b** *That person is really dishy (sl.).* ____________
- **c** *What a player.* ____________
- **d** *Hey, babe (sl.)!* ____________
- **e** *That one's a little too busty (fam.) for my taste.* ____________
- **f** *That guy is a really smart dresser.* ____________
- **g** *That person is a really good-looking chap (fam.).* ____________
- **h** *That person is my friend.* ____________
- **i** *Let me introduce you to my girlfriend.* ____________
- **j** *This is my fiancée.* ____________
- **k** *What a lovely bird.* ____________
- **l** *I see a real dish (sl.) over there.* ____________
- **m** *This is my husband.* ____________

Lösung 49 **a** *involved with* **b** *had a boyfriend already* **c** *left* **d** *chat Rachel up (fam.)* **e** *gave him a chance* **f** *kissed* **g** *got what he wanted* **h** *crazy about him* **i** *deeply in love* **j** *day one* **k** *get serious* **l** *possessive* **m** *stop looking at*

Each sentence has an incorrect preposition. Underline the incorrect preposition and replace it by the correct one!

51

- a) *Tom was slowly getting fed up (fam.) on Rachel's jealousy.* ________
- b) *Within weeks they had had enough for each other.* ________
- c) *Neither of them wanted to break down.* ________
- d) *Rachel decided it was worth keeping in her efforts.* ________
- e) *He, too, wasn't ready to split off.* ________
- f) *The two lovebirds kept holding over to what they had.* ________
- g) *All they needed was time of their love to work.* ________
- h) *And it worked for a while, but only in and off.* ________
- i) *Both Rachel and Tom worked hard for their relationship.* ________
- j) *Tom was the first to call it up.* ________
- k) *So they agreed to spend some time up from each other.* ________
- l) *Finally, both ended down broken-hearted.* ________

Lösung 52

a *together* **b** *themselves* **c** *their* **d** *themselves* **e** *herself* **f** *for* **g** *around*
h *another* **i** *still* **j** *with themselves* **k** *together* **l** *apart* **m** *sorrowfully*

Cross out the word(s) that is/are not necessary!

a) *Some time later Rachel and Tom met together again.*
b) *The minute they saw each other themselves their passions ignited.*
c) *Holding their hands, they walked along the street.*
d) *Then, that great moment came: they kissed themselves.*
e) *Rachel wondered herself if Tom was ready to commit himself.*
f) *Rachel told Tom she loved for him.*
g) *Tom said that around this time they would make it work.*
h) *Rachel had another changed – she was no longer jealous.*
i) *But Tom still was still the same – always looking at other girls.*
j) *This finally led to their breaking up with themselves again.*
k) *One day they argued together.*
l) *Next, they went their separate ways apart.*
m) *Both felt very sorrowfully sad.*

Lösung 51

a *on – with* **b** *for – of* **c** *down – up* **d** *in – up* **e** *off – up* **f** *over – on*
g *of – for* **h** *in – on* **i** *for – on* **j** *up – off* **k** *up – away* **l** *down – up*

Romance – getting started, flirting

When we talk about love and romance, we use a lot of slang and other informal language. You won't usually hear an English-speaker say something like *They initiated a relationship, but they put an end to it soon afterwards.* Instead they would say something like *They started going out together, but they broke up soon afterwards.*

A common way of starting a conversation with someone you're romantically interested in is with a *chat-up line (fam.)* ("Anmachspruch", fam.) and the person who starts the conversation is *chatting up* ("anmachen") the other person. The opening remarks can be quite simple, the traditional one being *Haven't we met somewhere before?* ("Haben wir uns nicht schon einmal gesehen?"). There are also more complex chat-up lines which include plays on words, idioms and jokes, such as *Is it hot in here, or is it just you?* ("Ist es hier drin so heiß oder bist du das?"). And when you flatter someone and tell them how nice they are, you are *sweet-talking (fam.)* them ("Süßholz raspeln"/"schmeicheln", fam.).

A *date* is a meeting between two people who are romantically interested in each other. If they carry on meeting each other, they are *dating* or *going out together* ("mit jemandem gehen/zusammen sein").

Romance – breaking up

To *break up with someone* means "mit jemandem Schluss machen". It is difficult to do this without emotion and, often, bitterness and as a result breaking up often involves using direct and impolite expressions.

A *break-up* ("Trennung") might happen because one of the people in a relationship is too *possessive* ("besitzergreifend"), so the other person *needs some space/room* for himself or herself ("Freiraum benötigen").
Cheating on someone ("jemanden betrügen") is also a common reason for ending a relationship. Or a relationship might end for the more general reason that *it just didn't work out* ("Es hat einfach nicht geklappt.").

A common cliché used by people who are breaking up with someone else is *It's not your fault, it's mine.* ("Es liegt nicht an dir, sondern an mir.").
After the break-up, the person who was *dumped (fam.)* ("fallen gelassen werden", fam.) has to take time to *get over it* ("darüber hinwegkommen"). After being dumped, someone might quickly start a new relationship with someone else. In this situation we say that he or she started the relationship *on the rebound.*

53

Complete each sentence with the correct preposition!

a) I sent my CV ________ the company last week.

b) I've applied ________ a new job.

c) I've been offered a job ________ a flight attendant.

d) One of the customers complained ________ me to my boss.

e) He's always ordering everybody ________.

f) There's an extra five per cent commission ________ it for you.

g) They told me to sign ________ the dotted line if I wanted the job.

h) I was away for a fortnight, but now I'm back ________ work.

i) We have to adhere ________ a pretty strict dress code.

j) As I always say: business ________ pleasure!

k) They might offer you a post ________ a lower level.

l) I'm looking for a post where I can put my skills ________ practice.

m) My company's not doing so well. We always seem to be ________ the red.

Lösung 54 **a** *bend* **b** *appreciated* **c** *dirty work* **d** *in charge* **e** *way up* **f** *stopping* **g** *hire*

Use the words to complete the dialogue between John Smith and his colleague!

54

a	*Arthur: Our boss is really driving me round the ______________ (fam.)!*	quit
b	*John: Why? Don't you feel ______________ any more?*	in charge
c	*That's just it. He's always making me do his ______________.*	layer
d	*Well, he's the one ______________. He makes the big decisions.*	CV
e	*I want to make decisions too. I want to work my ______________.*	dirty work
f	*So what's ______________ you?*	notice
g	*He refuses to ______________ any new employees.*	rise
h	*Well, there have been a lot of ______________ recently.*	bend
i	*That's true. A whole ______________ of management has been cut.*	stopping
j	*Would you be happy if he gave you a pay ______________?*	hire
k	*Not really. I think I might just ______________.*	appreciated
l	*Really? Have you handed in your ______________ yet?*	way up
m	*Not yet. But I've started writing up a new ______________.*	cutbacks

Lösung 53 **a** *to* **b** *for* **c** *as* **d** *about* **e** *about* **f** *on* **g** *on* **h** *at* **i** *to* **j** *before* **k** *at* **l** *into* **m** *in*

Cross the most appropriate response!

55

(a) *What kind of hours does Lisa work?*

❑ *It doesn't pay very well.* ❑ *It's a part-time job.* ❑ *She hasn't applied yet.*

(b) *He wanted to discuss something with me in confidence.*

❑ *Sounds like a good offer.* ❑ *You must've been angry.* ❑ *What was the secret?*

(c) *Have you broken the news to your wife yet?*

❑ *Yes, that's what it says.* ❑ *Yes, she's always been quite lazy.*

❑ *Yes, I told her I was laid off.*

(d) *What's the daily commute like?*

❑ *Only about 20 minutes.* ❑ *A fortnight.* ❑ *About £20 an hour.*

(e) *I got a £300 bonus for meeting the monthly sales target.*

❑ *Can you afford it?* ❑ *Well done!* ❑ *Where's the snag?*

(f) *Are there any fringe benefits?*

❑ *They got fired.* ❑ *There's a company car.* ❑ *We all take turns.*

Lösung 56 **a** *see a film* **b** *are you doing* **c** *telly (fam.)* **d** *couch potato (fam.)* **e** *meet up* **f** *sucks (sl.)* **g** *nosh (sl.)* **h** *amusement park* **i** *club* **j** *entertaining* **k** *seats*

Choose the phrase that has the same meaning as the German translation!

a	*Do you want to (einen Film anschauen), Rachel?*	◯	nightclub
b	*What (machst du) later?*	◯	curtains
c	*I'm going to watch a bit of (Glotze, fam.).*	◯	couch potato (fam.)
d	*Tom, you're such a (Dauerglotzer, fam.).*	◯	seats
e	*Where do you want to (uns treffen)?*	◯	entertaining
f	*This film (ist echt beschissen, sl.)!*	◯	sucks (sl.)
g	*Want to go out and grab some (Futter, sl.)?*	◯	open-air
h	*Let's meet tomorrow at the (Freizeitpark).*	◯	see a film
i	*We're going to a (Nachtlokal) tonight.*	◯	nosh (sl.)
j	*The musical was very (unterhaltsam).*	◯	are you doing
k	*We got the best (Sitzplätze) in the house.*	◯	amusement park
l	*Lisa saw a play at an (Freiluft) theatre.*	◯	meet up
m	*I was so excited when the (Vorhänge) opened.*	◯	telly (fam.)

Lösung 55

a *It's a part-time job.* **b** *What was the secret?* **c** *Yes, I told her I was laid off.* **d** *Only about 20 minutes.* **e** *Well done!* **f** *There's a company car.*

Where would you hear these sentences– sports event, theatre, box office, TV programme?

a	*And now, live, direct from our studios …*	________
b	*I got distracted. What's the score?*	________
c	*Excuse me sir, I think you're in my seat – orchestra, row five.*	________
d	*Sorry, this reservation is not longer valid.*	________
e	*It's a close race, ladies and gentlemen.*	________
f	*Goal! And it's all over, four to one!*	________
g	*Coming up after this commercial break …*	________
h	*The interval lasts about 15 minutes.*	________
i	*What a wonderful actor. He has such a stage presence.*	________
j	*Ah, "cancellation«. I thought you said "reservation«. Sorry.*	________
k	*Do you have any returns for tonight?*	________
l	*They're bringing on a substitute.*	________

Lösung 58

a *I'd like to see a film.* **b** *He's a very skilled actor.* **c** *The concert was entertaining.* **d** *My eyes were glued to the screen.* **e** *At the theatre there was a long queue.* **f** *The crowd went crazy about Cher.* **g** *People were shouting and booing.* **h** *The room sat hundreds of people.* **i** *All the tickets were sold out.* **j** *It was a box-office success.*

58

Which sentence is correct? Cross the right one!

a	❑ *I'd like to look at a film.*	❑ *I'd like to see a film.*
b	❑ *He's a very skilled actor.*	❑ *He's a very skilled actress.*
c	❑ *The concert was entertained.*	❑ *The concert was entertaining.*
d	❑ *My eyes were stuck on the screen.*	❑ *My eyes were glued to the screen.*
e	❑ *At the theatre there was a long queue.*	❑ *At the theatre they had a long queue.*
f	❑ *The crowd went crazy with Cher.*	❑ *The crowd went crazy about Cher.*
g	❑ *People were shouting and booing.*	❑ *People were making shouts and boos.*
h	❑ *The room sat hundreds of people.*	❑ *The room sat down people.*
i	❑ *All the tickets were sold out.*	❑ *All the tickets were a sell-out.*
j	❑ *It was a box-office success.*	❑ *It was a successful box office.*
k	❑ *The stadium was stampeded.*	❑ *There was a stampede at the stadium.*
l	❑ *I got the last seat.*	❑ *I got a seat at the last.*

Lösung 57 **a** *TV programme* **b** *sports event* **c** *theatre* **d** *box office* **e** *sports event* **f** *sports event* **g** *TV programme* **h** *theatre* **i** *theatre* **j** *box office* **k** *box office* **l** *sports event*

Talking about work

When you want to know about a person's job, you ask *What do you do (for a living)?* When people talk about how they *earn a living* ("seinen Lebensunterhalt verdienen"), it is more common for them to describe their job responsibilities rather than say job titles.

Benefits ("Leistungen") and *promotions* ("Beförderungen") are common topics of conversation. Benefits may include *health insurance* ("Krankenversicherung") and *bonuses* ("Gratifikationen", "Zulagen"). When you get promoted from one position to another, it's a sign that you're *moving up the ladder* ("die Karriereleiter hochklettern").

CV (pronounced 'cee vee') stands for *curriculum vitae* ("Lebenslauf").

If you've told your employer in a letter that you are leaving, you say that you've *handed in your notice* or *given notice* ("schriftlich kündigen").

An indirect way of saying *sign a contract* ("einen Vertrag unterschreiben") is *sign on the dotted line* or *sign on with a company.*

Some employees have to *clock in/on* ("stechen", fam.) so that they receive their *wages* ("Lohn"). Others earn a *fixed* or *basic salary* ("Gehalt").

Entertainment

Various forms of entertainment are very popular topics of conversation – both during and after the event. When people talk about the various kinds of entertainment they have experienced: *films, television, plays, dance performances, concerts, sports events*, etc, they discuss the quality of the event – *exciting, boring, brilliant, fascinating*, etc.

When asking people whether they enjoyed an event, people often ask:

How did you like it?	Wie hat es dir gefallen?

Remember that there are some special noun-verb word pairs for various forms of entertainment.

E.g. You *watch television, a sporting event* or *a film*, but you *go to a concert* or *the theatre* and you *visit a museum* or *art gallery*. Be careful when talking about museums – many people confuse the words *exhibit* ("Ausstellungsstück") and *exhibition* ("Ausstellung"). You *view an exhibition* and *look at an exhibit*.

At a performance or sports event, people *cheer* ("anfeuern") or *applaud* ("applaudieren") if they like what they see, and they *boo (fam.)* ("buhen", fam.) if they don't like it.

Choose the correct statement for each situation!

59

a *John is at work. His telephone display shows that someone is calling from England.*

- ❑ *Rightman Insurance, John Smith speaking.*
- ❑ *Rightman Insurance, Smith.*

b *The caller identifies himself as Dr King. John asks:*

- ❑ *How can I help you, Dr King?*
- ❑ *What is your desire, Doctor?*

c *Dr King wants to speak to John's boss, Mr Jones, who is not there. John says:*

- ❑ *I'm sorry, Mr Jones is not to talk.*
- ❑ *I'm sorry, Mr Jones isn't at his desk.*

d *John continues and says:*

- ❑ *Would you like to leave a message?*
- ❑ *Shall I write something down for you?*

Lösung 60 **a** *my mobile phone.* **b** *at the moment.* **c** *to you later.* **d** *any chance?* **e** *call you back?* **f** *not available.* **g** *Helen.* **h** *have him call me back.* **i** *leave a message?*

60

Match the beginning with the end of each sentence!

a	*You can reach me on ...*	◯	*through.*
b	*She's not in her office ...*	◯	*have him call me back.*
c	*I'll get back ...*	◯	*your call.*
d	*Is Lisa there, by ...*	◯	*to you later.*
e	*Shall I tell him to ...*	◯	*not available.*
f	*I'm afraid he's ...*	◯	*call you back?*
g	*This is ...*	◯	*some other time.*
h	*I wonder if you could ...*	◯	*Helen.*
i	*Would you like to ...*	◯	*any chance?*
j	*I'll try again ...*	◯	*at the moment.*
k	*Thanks for ...*	◯	*leave a message?*
l	*I'll put you ...*	◯	*my mobile phone.*

Lösung 59

a *Rightman Insurance, John Smith speaking.* **b** *How can I help you, Dr King?* **c** *I'm sorry, Mr Jones isn't at his desk.* **d** *Would you like to leave a message?*

Which expressions have the same meaning? Put them in pairs!

67

a *I'll connect you.*
b *Who's calling please?*
c *Hold the line.*
d *Can I take a message?*
e *I'll tell him you called.*
f *Try again later.*
g *I'm afraid she's not available.*
h *I'll let him know you rang.*
i *I'll put you through.*
j *One moment.*
k *I'm sorry, but she's not here.*
l *Would you like me to tell him anything?*
m *Call again another time.*
n *May I take your name?*

Lösung 62 **a** *speak* **b** *ask* **c** *is* **d** *is* **e** *are* **f** *going* **g** *got* **h** *wish* **i** *is* **j** *gone* **k** *planning* **l** *tell*

Complete the sentences by using the appropriate verbs!

Lisa Smith: Hello?

- **a** *Hello, may I ______________ to Tom, please?*
- **b** *May I ______________ who's calling?*
- **c** *This ______________ Helen.*
- **d** *Oh, hello Helen. This ______________ Tom's mother*
- **e** *Hi Mrs Smith. How ______________ you?*
- **f** *Fine, thanks. How's school ______________?*
- **g** *Not bad. But I've ______________ a big exam tomorrow.*
- **h** *I see. Well, I ______________ you lots of luck.*
- **i** *So, ______________ Tom there?*
- **j** *I'm afraid he's just ______________.*
- **k** *Do you know when he's ______________ to come home?*
- **l** *I'm not sure. But I'll ______________ him you called.*

Helen: *Thanks a lot. Bye.*

Lösung 61 **a**-*i* **b**-*n* **c**-*j* **d**-*l* **e**-*h* **f**-*m* **g**-*k*

Telephoning – hello and goodbye

When they answer the phone at home, English-speakers usually say *Hello.* They might also add *this is* ... and say their first name. But they would not normally use their surname, unless they are at work.

If someone tells you that they're *returning a call,* it means someone at your number phoned them earlier.

Well, ... is often used to express that you're going to end a call – or to show hesitation.

E.g. *Well, I guess I had better be going.*	Tja, ich vermute, ich sollte jetzt besser gehen.
Well, I'm not quite sure I can help you with that.	Also, ich bin mir nicht ganz sicher, ob ich dir dabei helfen kann.

It is common to say *goodbye, bye, bye now* or *bye-bye* two or three times at the end of a telephone conversation.

You don't say *Until soon.* You say *Talk to you soon.* or *See you soon.* ("Bis bald.").

Telephoning – useful phrases

When telephoning in English, you should be aware of the most common telephone expressions and phrases.

Starting a sentence with *I'll* ... is very common on the telephone.

E.g. *I'll tell him you called.*	Ich sage ihm Bescheid, dass Sie angerufen haben.
I'll call back later.	Ich rufe später noch einmal an.

In order to ask to speak to someone named Tom, say *Could I speak to Tom, please?* or the more informal *Is Tom there?*

If the caller is asking for someone who isn't available, ask *Can I take a message?* ("Kann ich etwas ausrichten?").

If you ask to be *connected with another person* ("mit jemandem verbunden werden"), but that person is telephoning with someone else, you will be told *The line is busy/engaged.* ("Die Leitung ist besetzt."). Then you may be asked *Would you like to hold (the line)?* ("Möchten Sie dranbleiben?").

How would you say these telephone numbers in English?

63

a) *0475* ____________________

b) *0044* ____________________

c) *7117* ____________________

d) *2800* ____________________

e) *0800* ____________________

f) *7451* ____________________

g) *221491* ____________________

h) *23009* ____________________

i) *707070* ____________________

j) *281111* ____________________

k) *200700* ____________________

l) *477735* ____________________

m) *1212* ____________________

Lösung 64 **a** *is engaged.* **b** *you waiting.* **c** *another line.* **d** *for a moment?* **e** *on a better line.* **f** *the wrong number.* **g** *connection.* **h** *on hold.* **i** *been cut off.* **j** *is terrible.*

Match the beginning with the end of each sentence!

a	I'm sorry, the line ...	◯	a recorded message.
b	Sorry to keep ...	◯	been cut off.
c	I'm afraid he's on ...	◯	the wrong number.
d	Would you please hold ...	◯	connects me to the wrong extension.
e	I'll call you back ...	◯	for a moment?
f	You must have dialled ...	◯	on a better line.
g	I'm sorry, this is a bad ...	◯	is engaged.
h	Let me put you ...	◯	you waiting.
i	We seem to have ...	◯	when driving.
j	The reception here ...	◯	is terrible.
k	I called earlier and left ...	◯	another line.
l	Don't use a mobile phone ...	◯	on hold.
m	Sometimes the operator ...	◯	connection.

Lösung 63

a *oh four seven five* **b** *double oh double four* **c** *seven double one seven* **d** *two eight double oh* **e** *oh eight hundred* **f** *seven four five one* **g** *double two one four nine one* **h** *two three double oh nine* **i** *seven oh seven oh seven oh* **j** *two eight double one double one* **k** *two double oh seven double oh* **l** *four treble seven three five* **m** *one two one two*

Rewrite the incorrect sentences correctly!

65

a) *Could you put me through to Mr Smith, please?* ______

b) *Hold on, let me get a pen.* ______

c) *I'm afraid he's on another line at the moment.* ______

d) *There must has been a mix-out.* ______

e) *Is this a good time to talk?* ______

f) *Was that M like Mary or N like Nellie?* ______

g) *Could you letter your name out for me?* ______

h) *Could you repeat that over, please?* ______

i) *Could you speak out a bit? I can't hear you.* ______

j) *Could I call you back in a few minutes?* ______

k) *Please hold for a moment. I have to take another call.* ______

l) *I hear you perfectly – you're as clear as water.* ______

Lösung 66

a *please* **b** *thank you* **c** *please* **d** *here you are* **e** *Here you are* **f** *Thank you* **g** *My pleasure* **h** *thank you* **i** *Here you are* **j** *thank you* **k** *please* **l** *here you are*

Complete each sentence with *please, thank you, my pleasure* or *here you are*!

a) *Could I have some more chocolate, ________________?*

b) *What a lovely present! ________________ very much!*

c) *Would you ________________ leave me alone?*

d) *Who ordered the ham sandwich? OK, ________________.*

e) *Would you like to sit in my chair? ________________!*

f) *________________ for your kind words.*

g) *________________ – it was no trouble at all.*

h) *I don't know how I can ever ________________.*

i) *________________ – two beers and one lemonade for you.*

j) *I don't want any more, ________________.*

k) *You seem to think you can do as you ________________.*

l) *You said you would come and ________________.*

Lösung 65

a *correct* **b** *correct* **c** *correct* **d** *There must have been a mix-up.* **e** *correct* **f** *Was that M for Mary or N for Nellie?* **g** *Could you spell your name (out) for me?* **h** *Could you repeat that, please?* **i** *Could you speak up a bit? I can't hear you.* **j** *correct* **k** *correct* **l** *I hear you perfectly. You're as clear as crystal.*

Rewrite the words to write polite sentences!

67

(a) *appreciate it/if/I/help me/you could/would/.*

(b) *possible/send/as soon/as/please/ the package/.*

(c) *I'm/unavailable/he's/at/the moment/afraid/.*

(d) *what the/do you/know/to/happen/is/date/?*

(e) *to/any/contact me/hesitate/time/don't /.*

(f) *will/a minute/in/Mr Smith/with you/be/.*

Lösung 68 **a** *to write* **b** *helping* **c** *call* **d** *to know* **e** *took* **f** *wonder/was wondering/ wondered* **g** *to do* **h** *hand* **i** *to meet* **j** *to do* **k** *open* **l** *borrow*

Write the correct form of each verb in the requests!

a	*Could I ask you ______________ a letter for me?*	do
b	*Would you mind ______________ me with the housework?*	hand
c	*Would you do me a favour and ______________ me when you've finished?*	take
d	*Do you happen ______________ what the time is?*	open
e	*Would it be alright if I ______________ care of this tomorrow?*	know
f	*I ______________ if you might be willing to carry this.*	help
g	*Would you be able ______________ that for me?*	borrow
h	*Could you ______________ me that cup over there?*	wonder
i	*Would it be possible ______________ next week?*	do
j	*Would you be able ______________ that for me?*	meet
k	*Would you mind if I ______________ the window?*	write
l	*Could I ______________ your newspaper?*	call

Lösung 67

a *I would appreciate it if you could help me.* **b** *Please send the package as soon as possible.* **c** *I'm afraid he's unavailable at the moment.* **d** *Do you happen to know what the date is?* **e** *Don't hesitate to contact me any time.* **f** *Mr Smith will be with you in a minute.*

Telephoning – problems

When checking English spelling over the telephone, there is no fixed way of referring to letters as there is in German. English-speakers use names to try to make the spelling clear, or they might use place names or common words or even jokes.

E.g. Tom – *T for two, O for orange, M for Mary*
Helen – *H for Harriet, E as in elephant, L for leather, E as in elephant, N for Nancy*
But, make sure you don't say *N 'like' Nancy* ("N wie Nancy").

The figures in phone numbers are spoken as separate numbers, pausing after groups of three, four or five – but not two. If two figures are repeated, people often say *double*. For *O*, say *oh* or *zero*.

If you're having trouble hearing someone, you may have a *bad line/connection* ("Verbindung") or *bad reception* ("Empfang"). If you and your conversation partner are *cut off* ("getrennt werden"), call back right away and apologize – even if it wasn't your fault. It's also important to apologize if you've *dialled the wrong number* ("sich verwählen") or if the *operator* ("Telefonist(-in)") connects you to the wrong *extension* ("Durchwahl").

Politeness

Phrases using the continuous form in the past tense (e.g. *I was wondering/hoping ...*) are commonly used when making requests. This makes what you are saying sound more polite and less direct.

You can soften bad news by starting your sentence with *I'm afraid ...* or *I'm sorry to say ...* . *Just* is a useful word for softening requests.

E.g. *I was just wondering if ...* Ich wollte nur fragen, ob ...

Maybe is also a very helpful word, particularly for suggestions.

E.g. *Maybe we should consider something else.* Vielleicht sollten wir etwas anderes in Erwägung ziehen.

Remember, there are several different translations for "Bitte". If you are making a request, you say *Please*. If someone has done something or given you something nice, you say *Thank you*. If someone has thanked you, there are several possible replies, e.g. *It was a pleasure.* or *Don't mention it.* or, in America, *You're welcome.*

Choose the word that completes each euphemism correctly!

a	*They slept in the same bed. Do you think they ________ it (fam.)?*	with
b	*Sue and Tara finally came out of the ________.*	wash
c	*I'm sorry to say he's ________ away.*	did
d	*The firm decided to ________ him go.*	closet
e	*My grandfather is no longer ________ us.*	citizen
f	*I have to spend a ________ (sl.).*	collateral
g	*He has very little money. He's economically ________.*	deprived
h	*He's not stupid, he's mentally ________.*	substance
i	*At age 65, you're officially a senior ________.*	penny
j	*She's not an addict, she's a ________ abuser.*	let
k	*Where's the toilet? I need to ________ my hands.*	influence
l	*The military officers reported the ________ damage.*	passed
m	*He's not drunk, he's under the ________ of alcohol.*	challenged

Lösung 70 **a** *sick* **b** *died* **c** *fired* **d** *use the toilet* **e** *toilet* **f** *handicapped* **g** *unattractive* **h** *dustman* **i** *old* **j** *shit* **k** *having sex* **l** *pornographic* **m** *fat*

Choose the word/phrase with the same meaning as the marked phrase!

a	*She's* ***under the weather****.*	◯	old
b	*He* ***passed away****.*	◯	pornographic
c	*I was* ***given the sack****.*	◯	unattractive
d	*I have to* ***wash my hands****.*	◯	died
e	*Where's the* ***gents****?*	◯	fat
f	*He's* ***physically challenged****.*	◯	poo
g	*She's* ***rather a plain Jane****.*	◯	sick
h	*He's a* ***refuse collector****.*	◯	use the toilet
i	*She's* ***getting on in years****.*	◯	dustman
j	*The streets are covered in dog* ***dirt****.*	◯	toilet
k	*I could hear the neighbours* ***making love****.*	◯	fired
l	*He enjoys reading* ***adult*** *magazines.*	◯	handicapped
m	*He's a bit* ***on the chubby side****.*	◯	having sex

Lösung 69
a *did* **b** *closet* **c** *passed* **d** *let* **e** *with* **f** *penny* **g** *deprived* **h** *challenged*
i *citizen* **j** *substance* **k** *wash* **l** *collateral* **m** *influence*

71

Which option is not a euphemism?

a
- ❑ *The company had to let some employees go.*
- ❑ *The company had to fire some of their employees.*

b
- ❑ *Tom was economical with the truth.*
- ❑ *Tom told lies.*

c
- ❑ *Oh, my goodness!*
- ❑ *Oh, my God!*

d
- ❑ *He's a bit on the heavy side.*
- ❑ *He's a bit overweight.*

e
- ❑ *Jeez!*
- ❑ *Jesus!*

f
- ❑ *She likes to give money to the poor.*
- ❑ *She likes to give money to the underprivileged.*

g
- ❑ *She's a stewardess.*
- ❑ *She's a flight attendant.*

Lösung 72 **a** *skin* **b** *roof* **c** *thumb* **d** *footsteps* **e** *beans* **f** *sleeve* **g** *horse*

There are two options for each sentence. Choose the one that completes the sentence correctly!

72

a	*Beauty is only ____________ deep.* *(Schönheit ist nur an der Oberfläche.)*	skin/surface
b	*He went through the ____________.* *(Er ging vor Wut an die Decke.)*	roof/top
c	*The rule of ____________ is …* *(Die Faustregel ist …)*	fist/thumb
d	*He's following in his father's ____________.* *(Er tritt in die Fußstapfen seines Vaters.)*	footsteps/path
e	*She spilled the ____________.* *(Sie hat das Geheimnis preisgegeben.)*	story/beans
f	*I think she's got something up her ____________.* *(Ich glaube, sie hat etwas in petto.)*	sleeve/arm
g	*I could eat a ____________.* *(Ich habe einen Bärenhunger.)*	bear/horse

Lösung 71 **a** *The company had to fire some of their employees.* **b** *Tom told lies.* **c** *Oh, my God!* **d** *He's a bit overweight.* **e** *Jesus!* **f** *She likes to give money to the poor.* **g** *She's a stewardess.*

73

Match the beginning with the end of each idiom!

a	*It's OK. This time I'll let you …*	◯	*the hay.*
b	*What a relief! You got her just …*	◯	*green fingers.*
c	*You have my attention. I'm …*	◯	*hurt a fly.*
d	*Don't worry about it! It's …*	◯	*on her.*
e	*Tom's very nice. He wouldn't …*	◯	*off the hook.*
f	*What a beautiful garden. You have …*	◯	*eyes on her.*
g	*Lisa loves chocolate! She has a real …*	◯	*your breath.*
h	*I'm exhausted. It's time to hit …*	◯	*in the nick of time.*
i	*John fell in love with Lisa the moment he laid …*	◯	*in the bag.*
j	*Enough compliments! Stop trying to butter …*	◯	*the line.*
k	*Tom, be nice to your sister! Stop picking …*	◯	*sweet tooth.*
l	*I've already made my decision, so don't waste …*	◯	*all ears.*
m	*I've had enough of your nonsense. It's time to draw …*	◯	*me up.*

Lösung 74 **a** *mind* **b** *bear* **c** *basket* **d** *weight* **e** *plunge* **f** *class* **g** *nose* **h** *tight* **i** *edge* **i** *said* **k** *bush* **l** *fingers* **m** *bird*

74 Unscramble the marked word to complete the idioms!

a) *You've got to keep an open* ***dmin****.* ____________

b) *Stop complaining. Just grin and* ***raeb*** *it.* ____________

c) *It's risky to put all your eggs in one* ***tbkase****.* ____________

d) *Don't be so lazy. You've got to pull your own* ***ghtiew****.* ____________

e) *I'm going to take the* ***lupgen*** *and do what I've always dreamt of.* ____________

f) *Tom is a brilliant pupil. He's always at the top of his* ***slsca****.* ____________

g) *That looks expensive. You must have paid through the* ***snoe****.* ____________

h) *You sit* ***ghtit*** *right here and I'll be back in a minute.* ____________

i) *I was really nervous, so I was on* ***deeg*** *all night.* ____________

j) *You think I should leave my boyfriend? Easier* ***dias*** *than done.* ____________

k) *Don't beat around the* ***sbuh*** *– just say what you mean!* ____________

l) *Good luck! I'll keep my* ***fsinrge*** *crossed for you.* ____________

m) *As I always say, the early* ***bdir*** *catches the worm!* ____________

Lösung 73 **a** *off the hook.* **b** *in the nick of time.* **c** *all ears.* **d** *in the bag.* **e** *hurt a fly.* **f** *green fingers.* **g** *sweet tooth.* **h** *the hay.* **i** *eyes on her.* **j** *me up.* **k** *on her.* **l** *your breath.* **m** *the line.*

Euphemisms

Euphemisms are used in all languages – but those things which are euphemised and how they are euphemised, are culture-specific. Compared to German-speakers, English-speakers generally speak in a less direct way.

In America it is considered very impolite to use the word *toilet*, which is why you will see signs for and hear people asking for the *bathroom* or the *restroom*. This isn't the case in Britain, though. However, British people do often refer to the *ladies'* or the *gents'* or, in informal English, the *loo*.

There are many euphemisms for other unpleasant bodily functions.

Americans also tend to be more *politically correct* when talking about sensitive issues, such as job titles or cultural minorities. For example, "ein Schwarzer" is no longer called *a black* – he or she is an *African-American*. And "ein Müllmann" might be called *a sanitary engineer* instead of a *dustman*.

All English-speakers use euphemisms for death and dying. You will rarely hear *He's dead/dying*. Instead, people say 'nicer' things, like *He passed away/on*.

Idioms

Idiomatic expressions are combinations of words that cannot be translated word for word into another language. To reach an advanced level of English language skills you must be able to understand and use idioms. Many idioms are very similar in English and German.

E.g. *easier said than done*	leichter gesagt als getan
to let the cat out of the bag	die Katze aus dem Sack lassen

However, you must remember that most idioms and sayings are not the same and cannot be translated word for word.

E.g. *I could eat a horse.*	Ich habe einen Bärenhunger.
It's raining cats and dogs.	Es regnet Bindfäden.

The last three examples are some of many idioms that include animals.

Similar to idioms are *sayings* ("Sprichwörter"/"Redensarten"). A common way to introduce a saying is *As the saying goes* … ("Wie es so schön heißt …") or *As I always say* … ("Wie ich immer zu sagen pflege …").

Is the speaker expressing *agreement* or *disagreement*?

75

- a) *I share your opinion.* ____________
- b) *I feel the same way.* ____________
- c) *I'm not so sure about that.* ____________
- d) *You can say that again.* ____________
- e) *I wouldn't say so.* ____________
- f) *That much is certain.* ____________
- g) *You and I see eye to eye.* ____________
- h) *I'm not convinced.* ____________
- i) *That's rather doubtful.* ____________
- j) *Indeed.* ____________
- k) *You have a point there.* ____________
- l) *That's not the way I see it.* ____________
- m) *I'll buy that.* ____________

Lösung 76 **a** *my opinion.* **b** *like a sound argument.* **c** *see it, we have no chance.* **d** *that we must act now.* **e** *I still don't agree.* **f** *be the case.* **g** *of the question.* **h** *to eye, don't we?* **i** *true or*

Match the beginning with the end of each sentence!

a	*Not in ...*	◯	*I still don't agree.*
b	*That sounds ...*	◯	*to eye, don't we?*
c	*The way I ...*	◯	*true or not.*
d	*I am of the view ...*	◯	*to reason?*
e	*That's all very well, but ...*	◯	*that we must act now.*
f	*That seems to ...*	◯	*differ.*
g	*That's out ...*	◯	*thought about the topic.*
h	*You and I certainly see eye ..*	◯	*my opinion.*
i	*I'm still not sure whether that's ...*	◯	*be the case.*
j	*Would you just listen ...*	◯	*of the question.*
k	*I was wondering what you ...*	◯	*see it, we have no chance.*
l	*I'll buy ...*	◯	*like a sound argument.*
m	*I beg to ...*	◯	*that argument.*

76

Lösung 75

a *agreement* **b** *agreement* **c** *disagreement* **d** *agreement* **e** *disagreement* **f** *agreement* **g** *agreement* **h** *disagreement* **i** *disagreement* **j** *agreement* **k** *agreement* **l** *disagreement* **m** *agreement*

Agree with the following statements by writing *"So … I"* or *"Nor … I"*!

77

a) *I'm going to a birthday party at the weekend.* ________________

b) *I used to enjoy playing football.* ________________

c) *I can't sleep if I drink coffee after 8 p.m.* ________________

d) *I would have liked to go with them.* ________________

e) *I haven't been to London in a long time.* ________________

f) *I hate the taste of garlic.* ________________

g) *I don't like the smell of petrol.* ________________

h) *I might travel to Bermuda this summer.* ________________

i) *I shouldn't stay on the phone for too long.* ________________

j) *I will call Rachel this evening.* ________________

k) *I read the newspaper every day.* ________________

l) *I can speak French.* ________________

Lösung 78 **a** *Yes that's true, but only up to a point.* **b** *That's beside the point.* **c** *You've got to keep an open mind.* **d** *Don't talk back to me!* **e** *You're reading too much into her*

78

Rewrite the words in the correct order!

a) *only/that's/up to/yes/but/a point/true/.*

b) *point/the/that's/beside/.*

c) *an/got to/keep/you've/mind/open.*

d) *me/don't/back/to/talk/!*

e) *too much/you're/into/reading/story/her/.*

f) *hold/argument/your/doesn't/water/.*

Lösung 77 **a** *So am I.* **b** *So did I.* **c** *Nor can I.* **d** *So would I.* **e** *Nor have I.* **f** *So do I.* **g** *Nor do I.* **h** *So might I.* **i** *Nor should I.* **j** *So will I.* **k** *So do I.* **l** *So can I.*

Beginning with the first given sentence, put the argument between Tom and Rachel in the correct order!

79

Rachel: I can't believe what Sarah told me – you've been dating another girl!

- (a) *Sorry Tom, but I don't buy that.*
- (b) *Here's my reason, Tom – in my opinion, you're a big liar!*
- (c) *Before you start accusing me, would you just listen to my side of the story?*
- (d) *What other girl?*
- (e) *This isn't an excuse, it's the truth. Nothing happened between us!*
- (f) *To be honest, no, I don't trust you.*
- (g) *But I don't see any reason for you not to trust me.*
- (h) *You don't buy it? Don't you trust me any more?*
- (i) *Mary Jones. Sarah saw you at the cinema with her, three times!*
- (j) *I've heard all your excuses already, Tom.*
- (k) *That's not fair. I'm not a liar.*

____

Lösung 80 **a** *Tom's mum reminded him to mow the lawn.* **b** *He warned us not to enter the forest because it was dangerous.* **c** *Mrs Smith insisted on paying for dinner.* **d** *Rachel replied that she had not cleaned her*

80

Choose the correct verb from the right to rewrite each sentence!

a	*Tom's mum told him not to forget to mow the lawn.*	suggest
b	*He told us not to enter the forest because it was dangerous.*	reply
c	*Mrs Smith wouldn't let me pay for dinner.*	advise
d	*Rachel answered that she had not cleaned her room.*	remind
e	*John's boss said it might be a good idea to have the meeting on Monday.*	warn
f	*He told us we should ring for a doctor*	wonder
g	*John asked himself whether it was a good idea or not.*	insist

Lösung 79 a *6* b *10* c *3* d *1* e *5* f *8* g *9* h *7* i *2* j *4* k *11*

Arguments – agreeing and contradicting

You can agree with someone using the auxiliary verb *do* or using a modal verb the person said with the phrases *So … I.* or *Nor … I.*
Try not to say *I think that's not correct.* This is very direct and is placing your own opinion far higher than the statement made by the other person. It would be better to negate your own statement and say *I don't think that's correct.* or soften your statement even more and say *I'm not sure whether that's correct.* It's also polite to begin a negative comment with a positive statement. You may also soften a disagreement by introducing your statement with *In my opinion* …
("Meiner Meinung nach …").

E.g. *You have a valid point. However …*	Das ist ein stichhaltiges Argument. Aber …

There is no one word in English that has the same meaning as "doch". If you want to disagree with something that someone said, you must formulate it as follows: *I can't sing well. – Yes, you can.*

An informal way of saying you believe or agree with someone is *I'll buy that.*

Cross out the word(s) which is/are not necessary!

a) *I suggest that you to go home.*
b) *One should have to listen to advice from a friend.*
c) *I suggest that you must go home.*
d) *It's should advisable that we listen.*
e) *The lawyer counselled us to should go to court.*
f) *My advice is that we should to act fast.*
g) *I advise to have caution.*
h) *They propose that we might take the money.*
i) *Don't to go, that's my advice.*
j) *Would you advise us to should stay?*
k) *It might be better if we have listened.*
l) *If I were in your place, I would not to do that.*
m) *I think you might ought to call the police.*

Lösung 83

a *were* **b** *might* **c** *had* **d** *should* **e** *shouldn't* **f** *can* **g** *ought* **h** *pieces of advice* **i** *could* **j** *could be* **k** *make* **l** *might* **m** *should*

Studying at an English university

The language used for study purposes at an English university is generally more formal and grammatically correct than what you might hear on the streets or use with your close friends. If you plan to *study at* ("immatrikulieren an") a British university, you will have to choose a *main subject* ("Hauptfach") and find out if there are any *prerequisites* ("Voraussetzungen"/"Vorkenntnisse") you need to have before you *register* ("sich anmelden") for a course or seminar.

In English you don't *make* or *write an exam*. You *take, sit* or *do an exam* ("eine Prüfung schreiben"). You can either *pass* ("bestehen") or *fail* ("durchfallen", fam.) an exam.

When you *visit* a university, you stay there only a short time – a day or two. If you want to talk about the university where you're completing your studies, you say that you *go to* or *attend* a certain university. And when you want to say what you are studying, you can use the verb *to read*, e.g. *I'm reading history at Oxford.* ("Ich studiere Geschichte in Oxford.")

The word *university* is sometimes abbreviated to *varsity*, especially when talking about sporting events. Remember, "an der Universitat" is translated as *at university* – without the article *the*.

Giving advice

Remember, the word *advice* ("Rat(schlag)") is an uncountable noun. You can give someone a *bit/piece/word of advice* or *some advice*, but you can't give someone *advices*. People often begin giving advice by saying *If you want my advice* … ("Wenn du meinen Rat hören willst …").

The conditional expression *If I were you …* is quite common when giving advice. People sometimes also say *If I was you …* but this is considered incorrect in standard English.

E.g. *If I were you, I would ask him.* Wenn ich du wäre, würde ich ihn fragen.

Another common expression is *You'd (You had) better …*

E.g. *You'd better hurry.* Du solltest dich beeilen.

The auxiliary verb *ought* ("sollen") is often used when giving advice.

E.g. *You ought to see this film.* Diesen Film solltest du sehen.

The verb *must* is very strong. People giving advice often use *should* instead.

Rewrite each sentence, adding an auxiliary verb to add more emphasis!

85

(a) *She likes you!*

(b) *We need to get to the next town fast.*

(c) *Please sit down. Can I get you something?*

(d) *I don't exercise much now, but I played football when I was younger.*

(e) *However, they often travel at the weekend.*

(f) *Oh, I enjoy a nice cup of tea.*

(g) *I insist that you come with us.*

Lösung 86 **a** *In fact* **b** *Unfortunately* **c** *really* **d** *Actually* **e** *By the way* **f** *Surprisingly*

86

Choose the correct word or phrase to complete each sentence!

(a) *I don't think Tom will come back. ____________, I know he won't.*

In fact | By the way | Surprisingly

(b) *____________, I don't think I can come after all.*

Amazingly | Unfortunately | Ridiculously

(c) *Do you like this song? – Not ____________.*

actually | strangely | really

(d) *____________, I was thinking of doing something completely different.*

Actually | Understandably | Really

(e) *____________, I forgot to mention that Lisa is pregnant again.*

Sadly | By the way | However

(f) *____________, nothing bad happened, although we thought it would.*

Surprisingly | Does not | Quite

Lösung 85

a *She does like you!* **b** *We do need to get to the next town fast.* **c** *Please do sit down. Can I get you something?* **d** *I don't exercise much now, but I did play football when I was younger.* **e** *However, they do often travel at the weekend.* **f** *Oh, I do enjoy a nice cup of tea.* **g** *I do insist that you come with us.*

Match the beginning with the end of each sentence!

a	*I'm not sure …*	◯	*repeat that, please?*
b	*I don't follow …*	◯	*aiming at?*
c	*I didn't catch …*	◯	*sure I'm following you.*
d	*Could you speak a little …*	◯	*you correctly?*
e	*I'm sorry, I didn't …*	◯	*what you just said.*
f	*Could you …*	◯	*your point?*
g	*Did I understand …*	◯	*your reasoning.*
h	*Let me make …*	◯	*more slowly?*
i	*Could you make your argument …*	◯	*get that.*
j	*I don't …*	◯	*I follow you.*
k	*What's …*	◯	*get it.*
l	*What are you …*	◯	*a bit more defined?*

Lösung 88

a *I said I don't like this music at all.* **b** *I'm glad we understand each other.* **c** *Precisely.* **d** *No, I'm not giving anything away.* **e** *Then allow me to clarify.* **f** *Then let's go over it again.*

Choose the correct response to each statement!

a *Come again?*

- ❑ *I said I don't like this music at all.*
- ❑ *Sure, I don't mind.*

b *I think I know where you are coming from.*

- ❑ *I'm glad we understand each other.*
- ❑ *Why won't you listen to reason?*

c *Do you mean to say that's not the reason?*

- ❑ *That's an interesting point.*
- ❑ *Precisely.*

d *Maybe you could give me a hint.*

- ❑ *No, I'm not giving anything away.*
- ❑ *Of course, it's very interesting.*

e *That's still a bit too vague for me.*

- ❑ *Then make yourself clearer.*
- ❑ *Then allow me to clarify.*

f *Now you've lost me!*

- ❑ *Then let's go over it again.*
- ❑ *Go back to where you started, then.*

Lösung 87 **a** *I follow you.* **b** *your reasoning.* **c** *what you just said.* **d** *more slowly?* **e** *get that.* **f** *repeat that, please?* **g** *you correctly?* **h** *sure I'm following you.* **i** *a bit more defined?* **j** *get it.* **k** *your point?* **l** *aiming at?*

Adding emphasis

The word *quite* can mean either *to some degree* or *completely.*

E.g. *We work together quite well.*	Wir arbeiten ziemlich gut zusammen.
Are you quite sure about that?	Sind Sie da ganz sicher?

English-speakers often add the auxiliary *do* or *don't* before a verb to emphasize something in a positive or negative way, e.g. *I do want to come, really.* ("Ich will doch kommen, ehrlich.").

Another common way of adding emphasis to a statement is by using adverbs such as *amazingly, interestingly, actually* to introduce the statement. The expression *in fact* is also often used to add an element of surprise to statements.

E.g. *Tom's intelligent. In fact, he recently won an academic award.*	Tom ist intelligent. Neulich hat er sogar eine akademische Auszeichnung gewonnen.

In fact can also be used like "doch".

E.g. *I don't think you did it. – In fact, I did.*	Ich denke, Sie haben es nicht getan – Doch, habe ich.

Asking for clarification

Native English-speakers usually speak quite quickly and use a lot of informal language or slang. Therefore, it is important to know how to ask English-speakers to repeat or clarify things they have said. Communication problems may happen because you can't understand the English being spoken. In that case, these expressions are useful:

Could you speak up a bit/speak a bit louder?	Könnten Sie etwas lauter sprechen?
Could you speak a little more slowly, please?	Könnten Sie etwas langsamer sprechen?
Would you repeat that, please?	Würden Sie das bitte wiederholen?

The informal expression *Come again?* means *Would you say that again?*
Other ways of saying *understand* are *catch* and *get*. (E.g. *I didn't catch/get that.)*

However, you may have to ask for clarification not because of a language problem, but because you don't follow the speaker's logic. In this situation, a useful expression is:

Do you mean to say ...?	Wollen Sie damit sagen ...?

Which sentences or phrases would not be acceptable/understandable in a conversation?

89

- **a** ❑ *Hi, John. How you doing?*
- **b** ❑ *Fine, thanks. Are you doing?*
- **c** ❑ *Fine. I'm about to go shopping. Want to come?*
- **d** ❑ *I'm not sure. Any particular shops in mind?*
- **e** ❑ *Well, first I plan to the camera shop.*
- **f** ❑ *Good sounds. When go?*
- **g** ❑ *At a quarter past. Sound good to you?*
- **h** ❑ *Fine. I know a chap who might want to come too.*
- **i** ❑ *No problem. If you know anyone else who wants to come, tell them to join us.*
- **j** ❑ *OK. Me and him will meet you in a little while.*
- **k** ❑ *We see us then.*
- **l** ❑ *Alright. Later.*
- **m** ❑ *Cheerio.*

Lösung 90 **a** *want to* **b** *got to* **c** *kind of (am.)* **d** *isn't* **e** *what are you* **f** *going to* **g** *anything* **h** *try to* **i** *a* **j** *(I'll) see you later.* **k** *I* **l** *were* **m** *You're not*

90 Rewrite the grammatically incorrect or informal slang expressions in standard English!

(a) *I don't **wanna** go to work today.* __________

(b) *You've **gotta** stop making so much noise.* __________

(c) *The boy's **kinda** cute, really.* __________

(d) *It **ain't** easy to be good.* __________

(e) ***Whatcha** doing?* __________

(f) *That's not **gonna** happen!* __________

(g) *I don't know **nothing** about it.* __________

(h) *We **have to try** finish our work.* __________

(i) *It wasn't **no** problem.* __________

(j) ***Later**, OK?* __________

(k) *Who did it? – It was **me**.* __________

(l) *If I **was** you, I wouldn't do it.* __________

(m) ***Not** very angry, are you?* __________

Lösung 89 *The sentences that are not acceptable are:* **b** *(How are you doing?)* **e** *(Well, first I plan to go to the camera shop.)* **f** *(Sounds good. When are you going to go?)* **j** *(OK. He and I will meet you in a little while.)* **k** *(We'll see each other then.)*

Choose the word that has the same meaning as the marked slang expression!

97

a	*Those new trainers are really* ***ace****, Tom!*	exhausted
b	*What are you going to have for* ***afters****?*	food
c	*He went* ***bananas*** *when he heard the bad news.*	American
d	*You've got something on your* ***bum****.*	annoyed
e	*I'm absolutely* ***knackered****!*	good-looking
f	*I'm getting really* ***narked****.*	pimple
g	*Do you want to get some* ***nosh*** *with me?*	cool
h	*He's a very* ***laid-back*** *person.*	relaxed
i	*Who is that* ***guy*** *over there?*	crazy
j	*Helen is really* ***laid back****.*	bottom
k	*Tom has got a* ***spot*** *on his nose.*	boy/man
l	*I'm feeling very* ***lively*** *today.*	dessert
m	*My friend Sue is a* ***Yank****.*	energetic

Lösung 92

a *of bills* **b** *agent* **c** *neighbour* **d** *wardrobe* **e** *price* **f** *detached* **g** *flat*
h *market* **i** *lawn* **j** *yourself* **k** *hunting* **l** *floors* **m** *furnished*

Match the words from each column to form common expressions!

92

a	*inclusive*	◯	*lawn*
b	*estate*	◯	*floors*
c	*next-door*	◯	*price*
d	*built-in*	◯	*market*
e	*asking*	◯	*yourself*
f	*semi*	◯	*wardrobe*
g	*two-bedroom*	◯	*of bills*
h	*on the*	◯	*hunting*
i	*mow the*	◯	*detached*
j	*do-it-*	◯	*flat*
k	*flat-*	◯	*furnished*
l	*hardwood*	◯	*neighbour*
m	*fully*	◯	*agent*

Lösung 91

a *cool* **b** *dessert* **c** *crazy* **d** *bottom* **e** *exhausted* **f** *annoyed* **g** *food* **h** *relaxed* **i** *boy/man* **j** *good-looking* **k** *pimple* **l** *energetic* **m** *American*

93 In which room or part of the house do you do these things?

a	*take off your shoes after entering*	◯	kitchen
b	*cook*	◯	wash house
c	*watch television*	◯	bathroom
d	*sit in the sun*	◯	pantry
e	*sleep*	◯	children's room
f	*store food*	◯	dining room
g	*hang up your clothes*	◯	living room
h	*wash your hands*	◯	cellar
i	*store old furniture*	◯	attic
j	*eat meals*	◯	bedroom
k	*wash*	◯	patio
l	*check the central heating*	◯	wardrobe
m	*build model aeroplanes*	◯	hobby room
n	*play games*	◯	hall

Lösung 94

a *Our daughter is in the adjoining room.* **b** *The flat has been renovated recently.* **c** *The rent is £400 inclusive of bills.* **d** *It's in a very convenient location.* **e** *They moved to London after selling their old flat.* **f** *My roommate is moving out in a month.* **g** *I found a very small two-room flat.*

Put the words in the correct order!

a) *room/daughter/is/our/in/the/adjoining/.*

b) *been/recently/has/renovated/the flat/.*

c) *is/inclusive/of/£400/the/bills/rent/.*

d) *location/it's/very/in/convenient/a/.*

e) *to/they/after/selling/London/their/flat/old/moved/.*

f) *roommate/out/my/moving/in/is/month/a/.*

g) *flat/two-room/found/small/I/a/very/.*

Lösung 93 **a** *hall* **b** *kitchen* **c** *living room* **d** *patio* **e** *bedroom* **f** *pantry* **g** *wardrobe* **h** *bathroom* **i** *attic* **j** *dining room* **k** *wash house* **l** *cellar* **m** *hobby room* **n** *children's room*

Acceptable incorrect grammar

The rules of English grammar are much more flexible in spoken English than they are for written English. Most English conversations will include sentences that are not grammatically complete, e.g. *Good idea! = That is a good idea!*

In spoken English, the subject of a sentence is often left out.

E.g. *(You're) Not very hungry, are you?* (Du) Hast nicht viel Hunger, oder?

In questions, the verb *do* or phrases with *do* are often left out as well.

E.g. *(Do you) Want to come with me?* Wollen Sie mitkommen?

People often use *me* instead of *I* in sentences like *This is him and me.* instead of the grammatically correct *This is he and I.*

People often ignore subject-pronoun agreement in sentences with *someone* or *anyone.*

E.g. *When greeting someone, say 'hello' to them. Them* is used instead of *him or her.*

You may have difficulty understanding a native American English speaker because many phrases are pronounced as though they were one word.

E.g. *'wanna' = want to, 'gonna' = going to*

Talking about where you live

When people in the US and Britain talk about the size of a flat or house, they usually say the number of bedrooms, like a *two-bedroom flat.*

When written with a hyphen, *next-door* is an adjective. Without a hyphen, *next door* is another expression for the noun neighbours.

E.g. *The next-door neighbours are nice.*	Die Nachbarn nebenan sind nett.
Next door are having a party.	Die Nachbarn machen eine Party.

In these expressions, *door* refers to a house or building. If a neighbour lives three houses away from you, that neighbour lives *three doors along.*

When people *put* a house *on the market* ("zum Verkauf anbieten"), they usually contact an *estate agent* ("Immobilienmakler(in)") and establish an *asking price* ("Angebotspreis"). If you rent a flat, you'll have to pay *rent* ("Miete"), which is often *inclusive of bills* ("inklusive Nebenkosten").

In Britain and in the US the *lawn* ("Rasen") is often more important than a garden.

Translate the sentences into English, using question tags!

95

(a) *Du willst nicht mit uns kommen, oder?*

___

(b) *Du hast doch keinen Hunger, oder?*

___

(c) *Der Mann ist Wissenschaftler, nicht wahr?*

___

(d) *John soll nicht alles so ernst nehmen, gell?*

___

(e) *Du kannst gut singen, stimmt's?*

___

(f) *Sie könnte die Richtige sein, ne?*

___

Lösung 96 **a** *haven't you* **b** *isn't she* **c** *does she* **d** *haven't I* **e** *aren't I* **f** *do you* **g** *have you* **h** *don't they* **i** *is she* **j** *would you* **k** *don't you* **l** *doesn't she*

Add the correct question tag!

(a) *You've been here before, ____________________?*

(b) *John's wife is from London, ____________________?*

(c) *Rachel doesn't want to leave, ____________________?*

(d) *I've met you before, ____________________?*

(e) *I'm a very clever fellow, ____________________?*

(f) *You don't want to eat right now, ____________________?*

(g) *You and Lisa haven't met each other yet, ____________________?*

(h) *Tom and Helen think the world revolves around them, ____________________?*

(i) *Helen isn't serious about wanting to marry him, ____________________?*

(j) *You wouldn't like to do me a favour, ____________________?*

(k) *You work for an insurance company, ____________________?*

(l) *She reads a lot of books, ____________________?*

Lösung 95

a *You don't want to come with us, do you?* **b** *You're not hungry, are you?* **c** *The man is a scientist, isn't he?* **d** *John shouldn't take everything so seriously, should he?* **e** *You can sing well, can't you?* **f** *She could be the right one/person, couldn't she?*

Was the sentence probably spoken by a British or American person?

a) *He hasn't got any friends.* ____________

b) *I'm going on holiday at the weekend.* ____________

c) *He's gotten much better at playing tennis.* ____________

d) *Tom's in hospital with a broken leg.* ____________

e) *We lived on Main Street.* ____________

f) *Little Rachel loves to go into sweetshops.* ____________

g) *We decided to hire a car in Manchester.* ____________

h) *I already saw that movie.* ____________

i) *I have got a lot fatter this winter.* ____________

j) *Put your baggage in the trunk of the car.* ____________

k) *Do you have a car?* ____________

l) *My daughter isn't very good at maths.* ____________

m) *John decided to do it again.* ____________

Lösung 98 **a** *candy* **b** *vacation* **c** *lorry* **d** *lift* **e** *gasoline* **f** *pavement* **g** *fall* **h** *parking lot* **i** *flat* **j** *film* **k** *line* **l** *cooker*

Write the missing words in British or American English!

	British	American
a	*sweets*	______
b	*holiday*	______
c	______	*truck*
d	______	*elevator*
e	*petrol*	______
f	______	*sidewalk*
g	*autumn*	______
h	*car park*	______
i	______	*apartment*
j	______	*movie*
k	*queue*	______
l	______	*stove*

Lösung 97

a *British* **b** *British* **c** *American* **d** *British* **e** *American* **f** *British* **g** *British* **h** *American* **i** *British* **j** *American* **k** *British* **l** *British* **m** *British*

Replace the British-English words with the American-English words from the right!

a	*Please buy me a **packet** of cigarettes.*	◯	streetcar
b	*Rachel left her **rucksack** at school.*	◯	movie theater
c	*The **zip** on my jacket is stuck!*	◯	apartment
d	*One **return** ticket to Rome, please.*	◯	sidewalk
e	*It took me 20 minutes to get here by **tram**.*	◯	license plate
f	*The **number plate** is falling off of your car.*	◯	restroom
g	*I can't see a thing! Do you have a **torch**?*	◯	pack
h	*Could you please tell me where the **loo** is?*	◯	elevator
i	*I'll meet you at the **cinema** at 3 o'clock.*	◯	flashlight
j	*I took a nice walk along the **pavement**.*	◯	backpack
k	*Would you open up that **tin** of beans?*	◯	zipper
l	*Our **flat** is new.*	◯	round-trip
m	*The **lift** is out of order.*	◯	can

Lösung 100

a *I went on holiday last month.* **b** *I'm studying maths at university.* **c** *I think I'll take off my jumper.* **d** *Rachel eats biscuits and sweets.* **e** *Post this parcel for me.* **f** *Autumn begins in a fortnight.* **g** *What are you doing at the weekend?* **h** *I'll go to the chemist's.* **i** *Tom likes crisps and chips.* **j** *I've learnt a lot.*

7 Rewrite the American-English sentences in British-English!

(a) *I went on vacation last month.* ____________

(b) *I'm studying math at college.* ____________

(c) *I think I'll take off my sweater.* ____________

(d) *Rachel eats cookies and candy.* ____________

(e) *Mail this package for me.* ____________

(f) *Fall begins in two weeks.* ____________

(g) *What are you doing on the weekend?* ____________

(h) *I'll go to the drugstore.* ____________

(i) *Tom likes chips and French fries.* ____________

(j) *I've learned a lot.* ____________

(k) *The building has an elevator.* ____________

(l) *The neighbours protested the noise.* ____________

(m) *The car is out of gas.* ____________

Lösung 99 **a** *pack* **b** *backpack* **c** *zipper* **d** *round-trip* **e** *streetcar* **f** *license plate* **g** *flash-light* **h** *restroom* **i** *movie theater* **j** *sidewalk* **k** *can* **l** *apartment* **m** *elevator*

Question tags

German-speakers often use expressions like "… ne?", "… gell?", "… was?", "… oder?" and "… nicht wahr?" at the end of a statement or "… wohl …" in the sentence. In English, at the end of a statement you can't add *…or?* or *… not true?* in this way. Instead, English-speakers use *question tags*. Question tags are formed like this: The verb in the question tag is built up from the verb in the main sentence. If the main sentence is positive, the question tag is negative and the other way round.

E.g. *This is a lovely restaurant, isn't it?*	Dies ist ein schönes Restaurant, ne?
Your joke wasn't very funny, was it?	Dein Witz war nicht sehr witzig, gell?

When you say *I am* in the main sentence, you say *aren't I?* in the tag.

E.g. *I am always the last one, aren't I?*	Ich bin immer die letzte, nicht wahr?

Question tags can also be used to ask questions. These are formed by making a guess, and in the question tag asking if this guess was correct.

E.g. *You take credit cards, don't you?*	Sie nehmen doch Kreditkarten, oder?

British versus American English in conversation

Here are some of the basic differences between British and American conversational English. In British English, the present perfect is used to express an action that has occurred in the recent past that has an effect on the present moment. In American English, the simple past is also acceptable. E.g. A British speaker would say *I've just lost my key,* but never *I just lost my key.*

Have got is generally the preferred form to express possession in British English. *Have* is preferred in American English.

E.g. *I haven't got any.* (engl.); *I don't have any.* (am.)

The past participle of *get* is *got* in British English and *gotten* in American English.

Probably the major differences between British and American English lie in the choice of vocabulary, e.g. "Wohnung" = *flat* (engl.); *apartment* (am.)

There are also a few differences in preposition use, including *at* (engl.)/*on* (am.) *the weekend* and *in* (engl.)/*on* (am.) *a team.* Some words which are spelt the same or similarly are pronounced differently, e.g. *schedule.*

Abkürzungen

am.	Amerikanisches Englisch
e.g.	zum Beispiel
engl.	Britisches Englisch
etc	et cetera
fam.	Umgangssprache
jdm.	jemandem
jdn.	jemanden
jds.	jemandes
jmd.	jemand
o.s.	oneself
s.b.	somebody
sl.	Slang
s.o.	someone
s.th.	something
US	Amerika